THE AMERICAN LANDSCAPE

The Rockefeller Foundation awarded a grant to the Department of Landscape Architecture of the University of Pennsylvania for the purpose of enlarging the literature of the field. The preparation of *The American Landscape* was totally financed by the Rockefeller Foundation within the immediate supervision of Chadbourne Gilpatric.

THE AMERICAN LANDSCAPE
A CRITICAL VIEW BY IAN NAIRN
RANDOM HOUSE NEW YORK

The author wishes to acknowledge the *Architectural Forum* and William E. Cornelia for the photograph of the Alcoa Building on page 21; the *Architectural Forum* and Joe D. Price for the photograph of Price Tower on page 58; and Gordon Cullen, Helmut Jacoby and *Fortune* Magazine for the drawing on page 139, from *The Exploding Metropolis* by the Editors of *Fortune*.

The American Landscape

10056

THE AMERICAN LANDSCAPE

1 | INTRODUCTION

The only object of this book is to make the environment and hence life itself more exciting, humane and expressive. It is not a book about good design as such, it is not a book about preservation or tidy-mindedness, and it is certainly not a planner's textbook with figures and tables and standards. What it tries to show in the simplest way is what happens to objects when they are set down together in the environment, the way in which they can be experienced by the people who use them, the way in which they have a potential for grandeur or mystery so often translated in fact into squalor or boredom. This is a book about the art of the environment, the art of placing objects together so that the result is something better than any of the original elements; the art of giving identity to places and hence to the people living in them. A new art needs a new name, and this one is called townscape.

In fact, of course, it is not new, only ignored or unrecognized. Men have always tried to make their towns expressive of the life inside them. In the Middle Ages the urge was as unconscious as the urge which made every church into an expression of religious feeling. In the Renaissance, men thought they had discovered the rules for this expression—simple, lucid and geometrical. What they had in fact discovered was the first few words of a language. By 1800, a few designers, such as John Nash in England, could speak it fluently. But then the Industrial Revolution came, and any thought of visual progress was swamped under more pressing needs—social, political, economic. Where expression or amenity was needed, the ideas of the Renaissance were used in ever broader and more grandiose forms.

And there we rest. We have an empirical modern architecture based (ostensibly, anyway) on specific needs, individual solutions, the creation of a humane and exciting environment, but we have no modern townscape to go with it, nothing to join up the individual masterpieces into a corporate place. On Park Avenue, New York, two undoubted masterpieces nod at one another across the street, each elegantly and humanely designed within its boundaries. But separating the Lever and Seagram buildings are a rush of cars, browbeaten shrubs, dumb pavements—a chaos of nonrelation. They remain architectural gems; but as attempts to be anything more, any part of the total city, they are stillborn.

This chaos of nonrelation is probably worse in America than anywhere else in the world. And this is odd, because most of the fifty states have created for most of their members the world's richest society. Nowhere else, ever, has the man in the street had so much money and so much leisure in which to spend it. Everywhere, interest in the arts is booming: yet the most continuous, most down to earth, most easily apprehended art of all—the art of making a pattern in the environment—is entirely neglected. It often exists inside a house, or up to the garden boundaries, but almost never beyond them. The job of this book is to take the eye over the garden boundaries out into the street, the parking lot, the gas station, and show how all these can be brought into relationship in purely twentieth-century terms. The whole land is waiting, to use or misuse as you will.

The intention is not, of course, to make each city into a pretty garden, with roses round the diner door. God forbid. Gardens where gardens are needed; industrial brutality, *terribilità*, canyon spaces and prairie spaces—each, too, where it is needed. This whole art of townscape is built on a fundamental principle—which can be a political and philosophical principle too—of the "is-ness" of parts: that each part of each city has its own specific character and that to give visible form and identity, this character must be expressed in its shape and pattern. The character may be anything you like, and the character may be sharply different from neighboring places—in fact, one of the keenest pleasures of townscape is the shock of contrast between two contiguous places with different patterns (the opposite of the endless drive through roadtown, when all places appear the same even though they aren't). Look at the glittering skyline of Detroit from across the river in humble Windsor, Ontario; look down from the decent quiet Duquesne Heights onto the roaring heart of Pittsburgh—if ever a city epitomized *terribilità*, in the sense of sheer Michelangelesque power, it is Pittsburgh; walk west from Lake Shore Drive in Chicago through streets as wildly different as the variety of a global *smörgåsbord*. The magic is beginning to work—the sense of the difference in places, however obscured or obstructed, will come through.

But surely all America is the same? Well, yes and no. On one level of course it is—the same paperbacks in the drugstores, the same kind of food in the Deep-Freeze, the same cars on the road. Yet in fact, this is largely a surface gloss of sameness, under which people and places are as different as ever: just as the roadtown of Gila Bend, Arizona, may look exactly like the roadtown of Trenton, New Jersey—yet New Jersey and Arizona are and always will be very different places. More than that, people will always want to feel different, to have individuality, just as at the same time they need to feel the same and part of the group. The problem is not to satisfy one or the other, but to satisfy both, simultaneously: the American environment satisfies the need for sameness completely, but does not begin to meet the urge to be individual. Even at the level already mentioned—the sameness of cars on the road—how else can you explain the need which drives the members of the proudest state in the Union to put on its indistinguishable Detroit-designed models, "Made in Texas by Texans"? This particular example is a kind of crux: because I am sure that a truly Texan car would neither look the same nor have the same performance or equipment

4

as a car from Michigan or Ohio. The physical needs are different; it is really a monstrous cramping of life's potentiality that they have to be satisfied by one standard solution. We understand this very well in appreciating the natural environment—the Grand Canyon, the Ozark caves, Niagara Falls are all extreme cases of individuality in landscape. Townscape is an extension of this into the man-made environment. Just one example. Pittsburgh and Cleveland are only a hundred miles apart, yet they are completely different in almost every way: site, function, temperament. But almost nothing has been done in the man-made environment to express any of this (H. H. Richardson did it in his Allegheny County Jail at Pittsburgh, where he created a three-way masterpiece—splendid as a building, splendid for its function, splendid in a specifically Pittsburgh way). In most cases the basic materials are still around, ready at hand, waiting to be expressed: townscape would make Pittsburgh more Pittsburgh-like, intensify the Cleveland-ness of Cleveland.

And the aim, always, would be to improve and intensify the quality of life. America can do, quantitatively, almost anything it wants. It must transmute the endless quantity into quality or it will sink and die: 1984 will come on it from inside.

Townscape depends on two things: relationship and identity. Relationship means making the parts of the environment fit together—the supermarket, the gas station, the car lots; identity is the recognition and enhancement of the specific needs and qualities that make one place different from another. And here, right at the start, a big warning: that no identity is better than a false one. The needs and qualities must be real, not artificially tickled-up. It is natural, if most of the environment has no visual identity (and in America it hasn't), to swing the other way and attempt to be fiercely individual or to escape into a romanticized past. But that way lies the Nemesis of Old Sturbridge and the other reconstructed New England villages, of imagining yourself to be ante-bellum (with all the ante-bellum food in the post-bellum Deep-Freeze) or 1920's or any other time but the present. It is all very well, but only as a children's game.

One example. Albuquerque, for my money, is one of the stupidest wastes of human endeavor on this earth. It occupies a magnificent site between the Rio Grande and the Rockies, it pays no attention whatsoever to either, but simply goes on sprawling and spewing across the countryside to an endless repetitive pattern: without relationship, without identity. Yet, if it is a fearful mess, it is at least an honest mess. I would if I had to make the choice—but what a choice! —prefer it to the fearful mock-Spanish affectations of Sante Fe, where about six genuine Spanish buildings are lost in a welter of fake Baroque gables and commercialized Indian art. Albuquerque is the honest whore, Sante Fe is the wife who cheats. Making a pattern out of the environment has got to be conscious—the days when it would come naturally are long past for the U.S.A.—but not self-conscious.

But, with that proviso, the sky is the limit. The job is enormous, and it is a good thing that America has reached the point where almost any material advance and convenience can be had for the asking. All that ingenuity and abundance which up to now has merely resulted in gibberish must be given a change of direction to make the visible world—town, country, exurb—whole again.

Aw, what the hell. Why bother? There's always more land around the corner. Making places look nice is fine-art stuff. Anyway, my own subdivision has flowers in the gardens, my own living room is neat and tidy. Anyway, America is too young and too busy getting ahead.

A common enough reaction: an understandable one. But a reaction of a thrice-blind man. Blind literally, in that he cannot see the sheer excitement of making a place expressive. A walk in a town can be as refreshing and exhilarating as Scotch-on-the-rocks after a hot, tiring day: all that is needed is to open one's eyes to a new dimension of enjoyment.

At the other end of the spectrum, blind to the fact that whatever view one takes of the purpose of life, man is certainly not the only creature on this planet, but part of a natural order which is larger than he is and which he ignores at his peril. Heedless, reckless, large-scale tampering with the environment is one of the easiest ways to upset this natural order, an exact parallel to the heedless, reckless misuse of antibiotics on the human body, which is a microcosm of the natural order.

Man is not alone in the world and he cannot push the environment around as he will; it will turn back at him and hit him—at its simplest, this is the moral of the dust bowls in the Panhandle. But nature can also operate in more complicated and subtle ways. The correlation, unconfirmed but undoubted, between lung cancer and the various gases twentieth-century man inhales into his lungs is one example.

The third dimension of blindness is psychological, halfway between the simple reaction to the outside world and the cosmic relationship to every other thing in the planet. I am not setting up as a psychologist, but it seems a commonplace that almost everyone is born with the need for identification with his surroundings and a relationship to them—with the need to be in a recognizable place. So, sense of place is not a fine-art extra, it is something which man cannot afford to do without. However happy the family, however pretty the subdivision, unless it is part of a bigger community that can recognize itself as being specific, different (in the same way that you recognize your own children), something is missing. Where the hell *are* you if you live in, say, one of the fearful **6**

anonymities around Greater Boston, or on a subdivision ten miles from a Carolina town, five miles in
the other direction from a school, two miles from a
supermarket? The complete fragmentation of the
whole man-made environment in this way is not a
liberation of life but an explosion, and it will end in
an equivalent fragmentation or disorientation inside
the personalities of its inhabitants.

By an unhappy series of accidents, a lot of America
has never really had any kind of man-made visual
pattern and identity, in the sense in which English
villages or German towns have. There is tremendous
local feeling, but it is quite unexpressed in the shape
of the place—or only expressed by functional accidents
like the grain elevators and the water towers and the
courthouse squares, grand though all these may be.
With "the towns where the automobile got there
first" there is not even that: around Van Horn in
Texas, or in parts of the Deep South like Mobile, and
of course in all the new settlements of the last twenty
years. With exurbia it is a little more understandable:
if you are way out on Long Island you do share,
vicariously, a little of the identity of metropolitan
New York. But more to the point are the brand-new
settlements. I want to describe just one: Grants on
US 66, between Albuquerque and Gallup. Now, Grants
advertises itself stridently and repeatedly to the passer-by as "the uranium capital of the world," which is
certainly something worth expressing and giving visible form to. And the site, where the desert runs into
the San Mateo mountains, is superb too. Even if
Grants is to be a short-lived mining camp, then it
should be the most exciting, most expressive mining
camp in the world. In the beat phrase, "get your kicks
on 'sixty-six' " (and what a mockery that is—US 66
has more potential excitements deadened and made
dull than any other road on earth), Grants ought to
be one of the kicks. And in fact Grants is just the same
old stuff as though it were New Grantville in Pennsylvania or El Granto in California. Everything is
flung on the landscape—which in a mining camp is
perhaps legitimate. My point is that it is no longer
flung with panache or passion, with a sense of the importance of the occasion. Virginia City, Nevada, is a
real place, whether it has people in it or not. But at
Grants this terrifying and exciting thing is reduced to
a genteel drooling and dribbling on the landscape, a
town gone visually 4F. In England I called this
mindless mixing up of all man-made objects without
any pattern of purpose or relationship by an invented
word, subtopia: in America it seems simpler and more
effective, more American, just to call it goop. Its
archetype is man treating the landscape as a set of
ruled squares and then filling them with low-intensity
muck. The air view of the approach to Phoenix,
Arizona, will do as well as any other to illustrate this.

On the ground—at the other end of the country, out-

AIR VIEW

GROUND VIEW There is no need to elaborate on this kind of view—to go over Paul Revere's ride from Boston to Lexington, for example, to see what the twentieth century has made of it. Put another way, almost everyone who acquires this book will have had to struggle through several miles of goop to get to bookshop or library. The problem is one that most people recognize. But the faults are not untidyness and brashness but universal propagation of lack of relationship and lack of identity. Hence the answer is not just a cleanup—that would merely give a genteel vacuum instead of a vulgar one—but a relearning of the physical laws of relationship and of the moral law that the same thing may not be valid everywhere: different places need different treatment. William Blake said it, as he said most things, in a very few words, and they might as well be the motto for the book:

> One law for the Lion & Ox is Oppression.

In other words, coexistence, recognition of departures from the norm, different environment for different types of people. Not an American Way of Life, second-rate, but a set of alternative American Ways of Life, all first-rate.

If some of these phrases, like coexistence, have become dirty words, I'm sorry. I didn't dirty them. And if readers cannot get behind the false faces put on words, they are unlikely to see in this book anything but what they expected to see anyway. If you go to the North End of Boston expecting to see slums, or to Pittsburgh expecting to see dirty industry, slums and dirty industry will be all you will get from them, and the best of luck to you: you may read town planning for a hundred years and never see the reality under the false faces of the "dirty words": that Boston's North End is one of the most human places in America, and that Pittsburgh is one of America's most exciting sites. The goal of this book could be described as giving each place, in its own terms and ways, the equivalent of the human excitement of the North End and the topographical excitement of Pittsburgh.

Excitement, kicks. If this begins to sound like a beat novel, it is no accident, and beatniks are in a way

8

the proof of the proposition that everyone needs, and in America few have got, a sense of place. Why else the journeys, the fetish for travel, feverish search for places which *are* places, a search so often unsuccessful in America—why go to San Diego? Apart from the sunshine, man has made it indistinguishable from Detroit. Hence the desperate relief in finding personal symbols of topographical identity in default of general ones, and the pathetic seeking of universal value in the Greyhound waiting room or the corner of State and Main. Kerouac's Denver is in his own mind a glory of excitement, a mixture of Amsterdam, Chartres and Naples. But why does it have to be in his own mind? What are you doing in this twentieth century with its unlimited means, *not* to make Denver the equivalent in excitement of Amsterdam, Chartres and Naples?

Kerouac's *On the Road* is even more explicit: back and forward across the States until fulfillment, at last, in real places—across the Mexican border. The touching, wholehearted acceptance of this pattern and vitality is as unbeat as anything I have ever read.

The beats are the reaction against placelessness in its purest form. But less extreme novelists show less overtly but more comprehensively the need and the lack of place. I am using novels here because American novels are as good as any in the world, and they work on purely American terms: what is wanted is that American towns should have the humanity, comprehensiveness, richness and excitement of the novels that are written about them. John O'Hara in *Ten North Frederick* and James Jones in *Some Came Running* describe and define places as well as people. Yet it had to be done purely in terms of people and the emotional change that they gave to those parts of the environment that are quite undifferentiated and indistinguishable in themselves—the Greyhound waiting room all over again. Gibbsville, Pennsylvania, and Parkman, Illinois, are places of tremendous identity and individuality, yet I am sure that they and their prototypes do not express any of this consciously. It is quite obviously not a question of there being nothing to express.

That was *then*, you might say, even if the "then" was 1950. How about the *now* of universal mobility where 20 per cent of American families move every year, where Los Angeles is five and a half hours from New York by Boeing 707, where the same house designs are put up in every state? These are remarkable statistics, but they do not alter the basic human needs. The forms they take may change radically, but the need is still there. To give one more literary example, the four families in John McPartland's *No Down Payment* are about as typically exurban as anything in America, and their subdivision in San Mateo County needs no elaboration. Yet they created in spite of anonymous surroundings and divergence of jobs an almost feverish sense of place. So in every subdivision in the country. And as the subdivisions get bigger and the distances get longer and the frustrations earned by man's ingenuity multiply (i.e., you can't find any goddam place to park the goddam car any goddam where), the longings for some kind of reality in men's hearts will get deeper and stronger and more insistent. And, perhaps, more anti-social. A rape or a murder is real enough.

Mobility, also, is not really relevant. People put down roots and need to put down roots in a terribly short time: I myself take about forty-eight hours, and it is something that you can test for yourself every time you go on a two-week vacation. I would even argue, paradoxically, that mobility increases the sense of place: and that this rapid movement of people is something a town must have if it isn't to wither away. Ports are living definitions of mobility, yet it does not stop them from being among the most individual of places.

What all this adds up to is the proposition that twentieth-century America has basically the same needs as fourteenth-century France or eighteenth-century England or any other golden age of place-making: it is just that it has lost the know-how to build places. The "why" remains the same; the "how" has to be rediscovered. It is the job of this book to suggest the "how": and to suggest it with only American examples. This has been a hard job, harder than it would have been anywhere else in the world. I drove ten thousand miles through the States, and what I found could have been turned up, in analogy and equivalent, in any two-hundred-mile journey in England. This is not Limey superciliousness but a simple expression of facts. If I weren't convinced of the bottomless, unexpressed need for an environment which is not perennial low-grade chaos, I could not bear to write this. If there is no human need, all the know-how in the world might as well be put on the bonfire.

In fact, I think there may be more need in America than anywhere else. Examples pop up unsolicited: in this morning's (English) newspaper in an account of goings-on in Tell City, Indiana, on the Ohio river between Louisville and Owensboro. There they held their first Factory Steam Whistle Concert—"We think it's the first time it's ever been done anywhere"—ending with a finale of "ten of the sweetest sounding whistles which could be found." America has a reputation for conformity, yet where else could such a splendidly nonconforming thing happen today? And what a terrific urban vitality that must premise—just the kind of directness that built Renaissance towns and Gothic churches: yet I am sure (I have not been there) that the surface appearance of Tell City, so different from the reality underneath, is like almost any other American river town—a brash gridiron half built up, turning its back on the river and greeting it, and the countryside at its edges, with all the junk it can muster.

2 | HOW IT HAPPENED

Goop, the goulash of environment, is not a simple thing due purely to the automobile or to exurbia or commercial pressures. The American mess is worse than any other mess in the world for a combination of reasons, all of which act together. Some of the reasons came over with Columbus, some are America's own contribution. They are like the components of an explosive that had been smoldering together for years and that finally went off after the Second World War. To get to a cure, the disease needs a more detailed diagnosis.

This has got to start with the Pueblo Indians. Do not be dismayed, gentlemen, this is not the thin end of an adobe wedge: the point is not going to be that we should live like Pueblo Indians, but that we should learn from them—and from everybody else—to enable us to live better as twentieth-century men. And the Pueblo Indians are one of America's few examples of the instinct for place-making that seems to be characteristic of natural man—man before the Fall, if you like, interpreting the Fall as man's complete and deliberate alienation from the natural order, which has finally been achieved in mid-twentieth-century America. The Renaissance and the Industrial Revolution were only harbingers of this: and there is no way back. From here out, man is on his own. The only way forward is for man to consciously remake himself into the natural order and to do that he is going to need all the help he can get. Hence Pueblo Indians will reappear in subsequent chapters, to illustrate by analogy.

So every man-made settlement in America was conscious and self-conscious. And self-conscious planning arrived in America in its most dogmatic and simpleminded form, the plane geometry of the Renaissance, the newfound simplicity which man thought was the key to the universe. Where better to demonstrate it than the New World? Now, Renaissance plans in Europe did not stay simple for very long: it was not, after all, the golden solution. And moreover, they were almost always next to or imposed upon medieval plans, so that the end result was not just formality, but formality plus informality, a very different thing. But in America the plans did not get more complex and more subtle: they got simpler. The progression was from the disarming strings of squares in Savannah and the quadrilateral of squares in Philadelphia to the single courthouse square of the Middle West and then, directly, to the straightforward gridiron. And at the gridiron, Renaissance aesthetic simplicity taken to its ultimate (rather like Malevich's white circle on a white square, alas), met land-surveyors' economic simplicity at its crudest. The grid was not only a kind of ideal, it was the cheapest and easiest way of carving up land. Like the Model T Ford, it ran its competitors out of business. But, unlike the Model T, its only virtue was commercial simplicity.

Like coexistence, the gridiron is now a loaded word. It has emotional overtones, it is supposed to be a typically American product like hominy grits or clam chowder, and it has the undoubted superficial virtue of being able to tell you in a strange town exactly how to get from Main and Seventh to Walnut and Sixteenth. Unfortunately, it is also the biggest agent in making all the blocks in between indistinguishable, because it has two incontrovertible drawbacks that are matters of optics, not of argument. One is that it decimates the variety available even within strictly geometrical and symmetrical plans—it is rather like planning a week's menu with veal, veal, veal and beef. The other is that it is a strip with no tease. All that you see, you see all at once—there is no more discovery, no possibility for continuous spatial experience, no come-on or around-the-corner, and this is absolutely disastrous to building up the shape of a place. Without such continuity, it is like trying to build a house with all the bricks but no mortar. One such street in a town is magnificent and maybe indispensable, but only as long as there are alternatives to it. Broad Street in Philadelphia seen either way is a splendid thing, whether focusing on William Penn from way up in the 5700 block, or standing under William Penn and looking out along a view that seems to stretch to the Canadian border. But when you have trudged around Locust and Pine and Walnut and found that they all seem to look like cut-rate editions of Broad Street, the effect begins to pall.

There have been plenty of reactions against the gridiron, starting in the garden with Downing and the layout of Central Park, through the Greenbelt towns to the average big subdivision of today. But in many ways, to continue the metaphor, these plans are tease without strip. It is a tragedy that American towns should be all formality in the center where some informality would harmonize and give point to the genuinely formal occasions, and all informality in the suburbs where a little formality is desperately needed to give cohesion and pattern.

And if the street pattern has no continuity, neither have the buildings lining it. I am putting forward continuity of some kind as a *sine qua non:* all it really means is that when I write a sentence, I hope that the words in it will bear some relation to each other: and it is the same with the parts of a town. They must make sense of some kind—which does not in the least mean regimentation or monotony, for I could have written any sort of sentence I pleased: it just implies some kind, any kind, of meaning—or even of non-meaning or chaos, but only as a special case. Chaos occasionally is good fun and essential: every life should have—occasionally—the completely aimless week and the helpless drinking bout and the sexual orgy. But chaos all the time is just chaos. A town full of permanently chaotic people is given a special name: lunatic asylum. Yet what else is US 1 between New York and Philadelphia but a topographical loony bin? And, like it or not, over the years places do react on people.

Each building is treated in isolation, nothing binds it to the next one: there is a complete failure in relationship—odd, in a nation which has self-consciously exalted family relationship, i.e., relationship inside the isolated units, to a new consciousness of "togetherness," and exalted it alas by such means that togetherness itself has become a dirty word. Yet togetherness in the landscape or townscape, like the coexistence of opposites, is essential.

What is odder is that outside the town centers there never seems to have been relationship of man-made units. To take this at its most revealing, a New England village green is not simply an English village green transplanted. The individual units are bigger, which makes the job of relationship more difficult, and they are already formalized and isolated as though they were a late-nineteenth-century suburb. What binds them together—just as in a suburb—is the trees, and hence if they are seen in winter, even showplaces like Ipswich, Connecticut, or Salem, Massachusetts, or Hancock, New Hampshire, seem flavorless, standing around like plucked chickens. In

SALEM an English green, if you took away all the foliage, the effect might be impaired but it would not be destroyed. Not that the New England villages are not delightful places; of course they are. But the point is that their charm is not really a man-made delight, that it is useless to go to New England for a solution even by analogy to our man-made problems. And what happened in the comparable parts of, say, Idaho was that the pattern was repeated first without the village green and then without the trees.

So, before the Industrial Revolution started and before it was possible to mass-produce houses or automobiles or anything else, the basic forces for non-relation and nonidentity were already there: a standardized community plan and lack of relationship between the parts. (I am trying to show just how the circumstances lined up to produce the catastrophic

13

exploding metropolis of the last ten years in America. The explosion is purely a twentieth-century phenomenon, but the reasons why it was catastrophic go back much further.)

In a country of small communities and small capacity for expansion this lack of relation may make life dull but will not make it desperate. Everything, after all, is still firmly anchored into the natural order. It is when mechanization and growth of population multiply, and thereby mechanize the means for creating this lack of relationship, that the trouble starts. So, in the nineteenth century, the fuse was begun to be laid, the infernal machine was being constructed. And, alas, America had one more ingredient to throw in: the perversion of the pioneering spirit which saw all nature as man's plaything, the entire environment as something to be carved up at will. The basis of this, I am sure, was fear—the great forests and rivers of America, perpetual reminders of something stronger than man: every inch of many of the early settlements had literally to be hacked out of the forest. So, shun the rivers, plow the forests, carve up the land with the simplest and most childish gesture possible, the pattern of squares—a gridiron applied to the whole environment. The degree to which this was carried out was in its naïveté barely credible: one personal example will show what I mean. Driving southwest from Detroit I had at last shaken off the metropolitan penumbra and was meandering along dirt roads well beyond Kalamazoo, with everything rural and—because of the Michigan barns, which will turn up later in the book—a delight to the eye. Comes an intersection and a signpost—a fine-drawn, elegant signpost: there are so many worth-while single objects in the American scene, but so few attempts to put them together to make anything collectively. When I stopped to look, the signpost said

SIGNPOST

14

Someone had actually solemnly carved a whole state into one repeating pattern irrespective of function, topography, or common sense. That was just heading for trouble, and we are just now finding out exactly what kind of trouble. It is the same thing, to give another personal example, that gave me the sight on my first day in America of half of a wooded hillside sliced away to make a supermarket. It was somewhere west of Newark on US 22, and it was one of the best days of the fall. The result was a terrible bit of butchery. Man is living in the whole world, not just on a billiard table exclusively populated by the two-legged creatures who protect their skins with such a strange and variable assortment of minerals. The butchery was unnecessary: the supermarket could have been built on that site and have been an enrichment, not a defacement, by exercise of the art of relationship. Man now has the whole earth at his fingertips, but his responsibilities to it increase with his powers over it. So much can be done if man—particularly American man—can live up to even part of the image he has of himself.

Being charitable, one could say that the pioneering spirit was responsible for "23rd Street and 52nd Avenue." It is mendaciously invoked to explain the mess existing between, say, Providence and Boston, an area where the last pioneering was done a considerable time ago. "America," they say, "is a young country, still branching out, it can't be bothered with all the niceties of expression."

Now, begging your pardon, I think this is nonsense. It is part of the ridiculous way in which man creates images of himself bearing no reality to things as they are. It is the mental equivalent of building a Saltbox or a replica of Westover to live in. (If it was taken a bit further, and people actually used eighteenth-century clothes and habits of mind and sanitation, life would at least be more interesting.) The bald fact is that the last real pioneering inside America finished when the railroad reached the West Coast: 1869. *Ninety-five years ago*, time enough for a smaller band of pioneers with much less means at their disposal, to build all the Norman cathedrals in England. America as a pioneering country, careless of details, is simply a bolthole for complacency. And in particular the idea of America needing to prove its manhood and virility by stamping on Nature as hard as possible, as a child might pull off insects' legs, is contemptible and shaming.

The attitudes and the accidents were building up over the centuries. All that the situation needed now was the means for explosion. The twentieth century provided them, like a two-stage rocket, with the automobile around 1920 and with the possibility for cheap universal mobility after 1945. But to blame the automobile or the wish to live in a suburb for the mess is a monstrous injustice. The mess is in men's minds: the agents only make it capable of realization. Northern

Switzerland, which is very nearly comparable to one of the "clean" industrial areas of America—say, exurban Boston or Palo Alto—has cars and suburbs, yet it is probably more exciting and interesting than it was half a century ago, rather than less. In other words, the products of technology have been used, not allowed to take command.

To all these factors there ought to be added one more. It is, I think, specifically American; and to an outsider it can only seem pointless and stupid. Its cause is natural and results from a misuse of the conception of freedom: its results are so patently absurd that any self-respecting society should have tried to control them. America is founded very properly on individual rights: the misuse is to assume that a business or corporation can act corporately as though it were, say, ten thousand individuals. It is not: it is another animal altogether, and one whose temper may be bad or good. If it is good, you get Olivetti of Milan; if it is bad, you get—well, take a walk down any highway. Because the billboards show the conflict between individual freedom and the common good at its crudest. Billboards, like the car and the FHA loan, are of course not bad things in themselves; they are just other means, to be used or misused. For man to put one sign outside his door is legitimate and logical (we in England have swung too far to the other extreme, and repress all such outdoor advertising that could enliven and humanize our urban streets). But for a company to act as ten thousand individuals and claim an equal right to put up ten thousand stereotyped signs in ten thousand different places is, literally, a perversion. It can be done, as the French do with St. Raphael or Dubonnet, by fitting each sign to the surroundings, by signing a contract with the site, as it were: by practicing the art of relationship. This can fairly claim the liberties of ten thousand individuals. But the same sign slapped down regardless of site from Oregon to Florida is just the blind, immature, unselective action of a spoiled child. And, which is doubtless more to the point, it doesn't even sell more X or Y or Z. (For me, and perhaps for more Americans than people realize, it sells less. I'm damned if I'm going to buy something that squats in front of my favorite view.) In Western Europe there is a wide variety of control over advertisements. Italy and Belgium are as bad as America; England and Switzerland have more or less stringent systems. Is anyone seriously going to say that the level of consumption of beer or gasoline, either over-all or of any particular brand, is less in England and Switzerland than in Italy or Belgium? Put in that way, the proposition is absurd.

This misuse operates in a vicious spiral. In the same way that you have to shout to be heard in a crowded room, so many standardized signs are visible on a main road, all canceling one another out, that the individual who has got something legitimate to say has to shriek it repeatedly. So, on US 66, through the

Ozarks southwest of St. Louis, a man has to say "Come to my cave" not once but fifty times, until you turn off the road in desperation—not to go to the caves but to get away from the signs advertising them.

An oversensitive, shrinking plant, this author? Nonsense. If you think so, it is your own senses that have got dulled, by precisely that amount. Apart from all this, stereotyped billboards have their place, they can be used, made into a valid, exciting part of the environment: a billboard doesn't suffer from Original Sin. But it must be used, grouped, related.

Looked at in another way, all this is an expression of conspicuous waste or the theory of obsolescence. And that in itself is another attitude which contributes to "the state of the nation"—the literal physical state of the nation's land surface—and why it is rapidly getting worse. Conspicuous waste, as applied in America, is a result of the misuse of mass production analogous to billboards resulting from the misuse of the idea of individual liberty. There are some things which are suited to rapid obsolescence and some which are not. In an economy which can make almost anything to any shape, size and degree of permanence, the dividing line is largely an emotional one. If a man is emotionally bound up with something, it is useless telling him that here is a brand-new XYZ and that his own XYZ is a heap of junk: he will continue to care for it long after it ought to have become a heap of junk, because it is part of himself. It applies to automobiles to some extent, depending on the quality of the excellence of the machinery (there is more feeling for and care of a ten-year-old car like the TD M.G. in America than in England) and it certainly applies to homes. To plan for an economy which replaces homes as one would replace electronic equipment is absurd because it ignores the emotional stake involved, something just as tangible as bricks and mortar. The moment a building is occupied it acquires—quite apart from its architectural quality—an emotional charge rather like an electric charge, something which in the end may be the most important thing about it. The continued existence of Carnegie Hall in New York, against all the odds, is an example of that.

What is needed is both transience and permanence, each adapted to the objects for which they are best suited. Again, coexistence: the simultaneous existence of opposites, the most important factor of identity, and the reason why the last few paragraphs have been wandering off the point to talk about the obsolescence of cars.

The misuse of liberty, the misunderstanding of mass production. There is a third element, more insidious, more American than either: the commercialization of emotional needs. In splitting and isolating in this way I am trying to make sense out of an imprecise but very tangible attitude that is a blend—often an indivisible blend, an amalgam—of all these and which is directly responsible for the look of the edges of Louisville or Cleveland. It is specifically American, but it is no more inherent or necessary or inevitable than the Prendergast political machine was to Kansas City. In its effects it is oddly similar to a corrupt city administration, and perhaps the same mixture of attitudes has produced both. What may seem to have been hopeless political morasses have in fact been cleaned up, usually by the efforts of one or two stubborn people. All that was needed was a starting point and an objective. The same is true of the visual morass. This book is an effort toward the creation of a lever: whether it can be applied to any fulcrum is a matter for America itself. And "cleaned up," of course, does not mean merely tidied up.

Of the three elements, the last is the worst. Its end result is that when you hear the words love or beauty or scenic splendor or elegance or charm you are sick to your guts. And that is a kind of living death, because all those words do in fact mean worth-while things. In visual terms it means that there is so much crap around that everything has to be super-marvelous to make up for it. As the next stage, the grafting on of emotional persuasion as a sales' gimmick (common enough from *New Yorker* advertising, evident also in the landscape)—feel as the Pilgrim Father did; take part vicariously in every kind of life—Indian, Mexican, eighteenth-century Virginian, imported European—but never take part in real life.

The end product is Disneyland, which is absolutely right where it is, i.e., as a fantasy world, a suspension of disbelief. The human mind and heart needs that, too. But in America, the attitude of Disneyland is being spread over the entire continent. This photograph on the coast near Hampton, New Hampshire, sums up the action and reaction, the goop and the gush, well enough.

The coast is the line of bungalows that marks out America so frighteningly to the air-borne visitor, all the way down to New York from the coast of Maine. And to counteract, New Hampshire has to call itself a "Land of Scenic Splendor." It is, indeed, but it won't be for very long if it simply trots out the inflated words and doesn't do anything to preserve the scenery. The same is true at the other end of America of the overadvertised Indian rugs in the astounding visual chaos that seems to happen anywhere in New Mexico where more than two people and a car are in one place at one time. The same is true, changing the sense a little, of exalting Savannah and Charleston as the apogees of gracious Southern living when both have Negro slums which would be surprising even in Naples. In every case the reality has been too squalid, so people have turned their backs on it and erected a make-believe world. Squalor has been compounded with hypocrisy.

HAMPTON

3 | RELATIONSHIP AND SEQUENCE

Hard words, but they had to be said. America has made the biggest hash of its environment in the history of the world, and there is no point in minimizing it. Enough is enough: nothing can be gained by reiteration. The point now is, what can be done about it?

The basic qualities that are going to be needed—whatever the scene, expressway or subdivision or city center—have already been stated: relationship and identity. The rest of the book will try and show what is meant by them, and will apply them to a few American problems. And it must be read, just as the landscape must be read, as an amalgam of words and pictures, each incomplete without the other. This is not a text with captioned illustrations, but a partnership of words and pictures in which on one page a photograph is used instead of a sentence; on the next description takes the place of a missing photograph.

Relationship is simply what you use every day of your life to make it coherent. What is proposed is an extension to the whole outside environment to make it coherent also. Relationship is what you practice when you drive a car crisply round a corner or make a ham omelette or put the rocks in the bourbon. It is simply the art of bringing together or operating on A and B so that the result is more than the sum of A and B separately. It is very easy. See first a building of several parts, actually one of the modern buildings by

WILLIAMSBURG AUDITORIUM

Harrison and Abramowitz that are such a pleasant complement to Colonial Williamsburg. This is made up of several different parts, and the parts have been related to one another just as the parts of a watch have to be related before the thing will tick. The result, the complete building, is more than the individual bits would have been strung out separately. (a + b) is more than a + b because a and b interact. And here is a pure example of nonrelation at its simplest—by the same architects, to keep the record quite straight—

ALCOA BUILDING

in the Alcoa Building at Pittsburgh. The skyscraper and the big glass porch, both good in themselves, do not relate in the slightest. The porch could have been in Cleveland while the tower stayed in Pittsburgh, and the architectural quality would not have altered a jot.

From the parts of one building, the next step is several buildings. The outstanding example, over at least half of America, is its barns, as splendid as the edges of American towns are horrible—yet just as modern, doing just as much of an industrial job and I am sure doing it more efficiently, i.e., with greater economy of means. They constitute the one great example of instinctive design in present-day America —design on the level of American jazz, that could also be the level of each town center and subdivision. The range can be simple: just the geometrical contrast of shed and silo—really the parts of a single building stated in an unexpectedly dramatic way.

NEAR NORTH EASTON, MASSACHUSETTS

21

Next, the interaction of one building, two sheds and a white painted fence; the fence is vitally important; the buildings by themselves are only part of the story, and in fact in this group this "identity" is almost spoiled by the other fence in the foreground with its unrelated set of verticals.

NEAR NEWFANE, VERMONT

Finally the complex interrelation of several units which is really a city center in miniature, worth at least as much of a visit as a house by Frank Lloyd Wright. Wren Oaks Farm near Dowagiac in southern Michigan:

WREN OAKS FARM

And in case the forms are too colonial, the date too early to be thought relevant, here is the same thing in corrugated iron in the remote and lovely countryside east of San Diego near the Mexican border. This insistence on barns is quite deliberate; they are the one approach that America has to a vernacular of design that comes from inside, and is not a top dressing controlled by the current architectural fad.

SAN DIEGO BARNS

The next step in relationship is from buildings serving one communal purpose to separate buildings expressing a communal spirit—the terraced town street. Not uniform design, which is the easy way out, but a consciousness of what is going on next door that does not involve any loss of individuality.

This street scene has to be old because we have lost the instinctive art of relationship shown here and have not yet learned how to create a modern equivalent consciously. The typical American Main Street makes the point all too clearly.

PROVIDENCE, RHODE ISLAND

This apology for a town center is at Pampa, Texas, but it could be one of a thousand others. Or, on a

PAMPA

NEW YORK SKYLINE

larger scale, the view almost anywhere in Manhattan, which is a continuous multiplication of nonrelation. It is exciting and splendid, but the point is that the excitement and splendor come in spite of the non-relation, not because of it. It could have been so much more exciting if someone thought about relationship. (Again, as a quick analogy, here are two tall buildings, which could as well be New York skyscrapers, in relationship to one another. Immediately it is like a chord, not two separate notes.)

NEWTON LE WILLOWS COLLIERY

24

Lack of relationship like Manhattan may produce nonsense, but at least the buildings are close together. When they are pulled apart (and in modern design they usually are pulled apart) without any replacement to bind the buildings together, all hope of unity or identity has gone, whether the architecture is lowbrow,

SUPERMARKET AT US 90/98

or highbrow.

HYDE PARK, CHICAGO

Yet it could so easily, without any surrender of American-ness or the twentieth century, become this:

ST. LOUIS

complex, intricate in shape and texture, a mixed grill instead of three sausages sparsely set on a plate. Notice how a movement of just a few feet changes the relationship completely. So in Venice or Rome: so, now, in one small corner of St. Louis.

Relationship can and must apply to everything, down to the smallest or most unlikely objects—just as it does in nature, just as a complex meal may depend on something as mundane as the proportion of salt. Consider a public toilet. Unromantic, incapable of being reconciled with a civilized, well-behaved environment? Not at all; what is needed is a bit of care, **26** and someone looking at the surroundings (and not with roses round the door or "ducks" and "drakes" either. If there is one thing worse than goop it is the gentility which puts frills onto ugliness in order to pretend that it isn't there). Here is how it has been done on the pier at San Clemente, a delightful small resort halfway between Los Angeles and San Diego.

SAN CLEMENTE

The appropriateness and tough elegance of this pair is I think self-evident: all done by a post and rail fence, unself-conscious design, and white paint. And they are, as well, self-expressive—they are more like public toilets, more themselves, than before. The whole environment needs to be made up of parts which are self-expressive in this way, a very different thing from applied "self-expression." The silly Viking-boat shape of the Yale ice hockey rink is a good enough example of that. The townscaper must shun it like the plague.

YALE ICE HOCKEY RINK

Emotion is not an artistic salad dressing. If it ain't there, don't force it.

And finally, to bring things literally nearer home, the end product of nonrelation, of a multitude of separate units, is the average big subdivision. This in a way is the core of the problem. If identity and character can be given to the Levittowns it can be given to anywhere—not because the Levittowns are worse than any other suburb, but because they show the problem of mobility or rootlessness at its most extreme. Here is a Levittown street (Levittown, Pennsylvania, in this instance).

LEVITTOWN STREET

The houses decently designed, the gardens neatly laid out—yet complete lack of coherence between the units, complete lack of identity in the whole. What to do? Undoubtedly part of the difficulty is a simple lack of building bulk: the buildings are too far apart and too small; there is not enough going on. This could be remedied on the estate layouts—smaller roads with a different traffic circulation, the same total area of space but arranged differently. But this is only a supernumerary difficulty. The main trouble is that nothing links up the units, and that the units are not placed in juxtaposition. For an exact parallel in terms of building size, go two thousand miles west to Ysleta pueblo, south of Albuquerque. Unfair? Not really: all the elements are in fact the same, except for the church —and one of the prime failures of the Levittowns is that what public buildings and shops there are are set apart, not integrated into the housing. Life is all one, and can never be compartmented; and neither can towns and goop. Yet in Ysleta there is a place, however dusty; there is a recognizable form that a man can look at and say, "I am here, in X. Outside is Y, somewhere different." In Levittown all he can usually say is, **28** "Where the hell am I?"

There is another thing here, too. The plan of Ysleta is an irregular central space with irregularly shaped spaces opening onto it. It is basically the standard courthouse square—but with a difference. The courthouse square is a regular opening in a regular plan. You can usually see it coming from a long way off, there is no build-up or surprise in getting there. Ysleta is very different. The approach along a narrow road, obviously with a hint of something bigger around the corner,

YSLETA

YSLETA

a few steps further, and one of the mission bell-turrets acts as a come-on

and tugs you irresistibly into the central space, where all is revealed.

YSLETA

It is not just an entry into a square, it is a complete spatial sequence. Space has ceased to be isolated, chopped up: it is part of a continuous pattern. Because of the relationship of its parts, the whole of a village is in relationship.

Perhaps examples are needed with a little less adobe in them. They are hard to find: most of them come from single buildings or building complexes; most of them come from universities where some sense of continuity (which is all that spatial relationship is) has come over from Europe along with the Gothic crockets and pinnacles. In every case, do not worry about the details, but read the descriptions as bits of narrative, so that a place becomes a continuous thing, a sequence of related parts. It is not any particular conclusion that is important, but the general knack of seeing all the parts of one environment together. As the *Architectural Review* once summed it up: one building is architecture, two buildings is townscape. There is no magical, specific solution here about what to do with traffic or subdivisions or slums: what is intended is a general solution to the way of looking at all these things so that the result has meaning.

The first example is purely American in a very American city—Dallas—and is a pure accident. Dallas is a gridiron city, but, by accident, it consists of a pair of gridirons at an angle to each other, and these meet at the exact point where the biggest and newest skyscrapers have been built. Because of this diagonal—and *only* because of this—a walk up this street in Dallas has all the excitement of unfolding and counterpoint of forms that should be the birthright of any big American city. The first distant view is immediately different from 99 per cent of American city views: there is something at the end of it.

DALLAS

At the join of the disparate grids, a building is set diagonally across the view: immediately it sets up a relationship with the smaller block in front of it and the medium skyscraper on its left. It fixes this corner of Dallas permanently and individually. Walk up the street, and the relationship is as mobile and subtle as a human relationship. A few yards further on, with the relative proportions only slightly different, there is an entirely different balance of tensions between the objects. Before, the view was a "there," a framed picture, something that could be viewed detached. Now it is jutting out into your consciousness—you no longer have the choice, to look or not to look. You can't help looking. And then, in another few yards, it is all over you, the whole visible world is the interplay of these gleaming up-to-date dinosaurs.

DALLAS

The eye casts around for a humane, messy, crappy anchor, something to reassure it. And, immediately to the right the typical American corner of the typical American street is at hand,

like the welcome jumble of a stenographer's handbag in an ultra-clean office. By itself it is one more piece of goop: in relation to the huge buildings above, it is a theorem about man and superman. Each is *necessary* to the other—the Golden Triangle in Pittsburgh has the tall blocks but no goop and is consequently dead. Again, in a few more yards, the two views come together,

and the result is sublime counterpoint, the quintessence of American-ness. Mathematical counterpoint of forms in the opposition of the two tall buildings, nose to nose; counterpoint of scale and feeling in the relation between unplanned, scrappy foreground and serene background. And basically it is all made possible by the intersection of two lines at an angle.

After that, inevitably, is anticlimax: how much more can you expect from an accident? The close-up of the ground floor promises something-around-the-corner—

DALLAS

but you follow in pursuit and are faced with blackness, emptiness, the familiar open-street view.

All that is the sheerest accident, although it is no no less exciting for being so. The next example is designed and controlled and calculated to the inch. It is in fact one single building, Paul Rudolph's Fine Art Center at Wellesley College; the sequence is the flight of steps that leads up under it to come out in the quad facing the Neo-Gothic buildings of a generation ago. This is, exactly, a microcosm of the problems that face—or ought to face—a town planner or town maker joining old to new, making the town a space for living in. The judgment and artistry and control shown by Rudolph here—for the spatial sequence is one of the great things in American architecture, New England's own Spanish Steps—are basically the qualities required by any city engineer who plans a new system of sidewalks. Every town alteration always has this potential and possibility: it can be inept, disparate, separate concrete and brick, or by exercising the art of relationship and sequence it can grow together into **33** an open-air work of art that needs no fine-art expertise to appreciate it. The alternative is worth taking; and in many of America's boom towns (Dallas, Houston, Los Angeles, Miami, Tulsa, Denver) the obstacle is not likely to be financial. This staircase could be any entry to any city hall or plaza, instead of the sterile marble pomposities that are usual. Any part of Philadelphia's Penn Center, which is decent but desperately dull and unimaginative, could have looked like this.

The sequence starts by being what seems to be simply a deeply inset entrance to the building.

WELLESLEY COLLEGE

That it is not, that there is something else beyond, is one of the fundamental tricks of this trade, a trade which in many ways is like the art of the striptease. Striptease is a matter of alternate tease and strip, tension between yes and no. After the qualified no of the first view comes a tantalizing yes as soon as you are on the axis,

WELLESLEY COLLEGE

when the entrance is seen to be steps, with, at the end, an entirely unexpected glimpse of a sunlit quad and other buildings beyond. Clearly, this is going somewhere. Good townscape is rarely a simple or single-minded thing, and two quite different sensations come in here to charm the passer-by. One is that the sidewalk in the foreground is gently V-shaped, gently sloping, leading the walker upstairs before he knows it (the opposite of the blunt uninvitingness of the stairs up from a subway. You go, emotionally speaking, only because the subway is more goddam unpleasant than the stairs—a balance of tensions indeed, but not a very desirable and humane one, and one which is more likely to produce enlarged ulcers than enlarged experience). The other point is simply the shadows made by the sunbreakers on the wall: the whole of sensual experience is the province of the townscaper. It need not even be visual experience and a few tiny pointers to this will appear later on in the book. And at least in those parts of a country which, like Albuquerque, register about 350 sunny days in the year, planning deliberate effects with shadows is at least as legitimate as planting deciduous trees. But nobody has thought of it; all around us are fantastic potential enlargements of our sensibilities and sensations, just waiting for us to use them.

I am sorry: we are some way from the stairs at Wellesley College. It is just that all environment and experience is indivisible, everything interacts or ought to. Up the few steps and the stairs have got us. Not the steps straight ahead, but the pair of staircases which seem to be descending about our ears.

WELLESLEY COLLEGE

These stairs are the visual equivalent of musical counterpoint, or an abrupt change of direction on a **35**

roller coaster. They cut into the whole forward pattern of motion—especially and cruelly in the exposed undersides of the treads, like seeing your own skeleton walking beside you. They are beautifully controlled—they only cut into the motion, hence enrich it, they do not stop it. Along the level a little further, up three more steps, along again (not quite so far, four paces instead of six; the pace is quickening, and

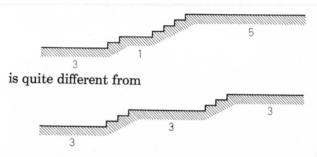

is quite different from

although both get to the same place with the same total number of units), up three more steps, with the buildings at the end visibly Neo-Gothic now (i.e., different from what we are in: "There" instead of "Here") and are just beginning to wind up and give the stairways impetus, when—Bang!—

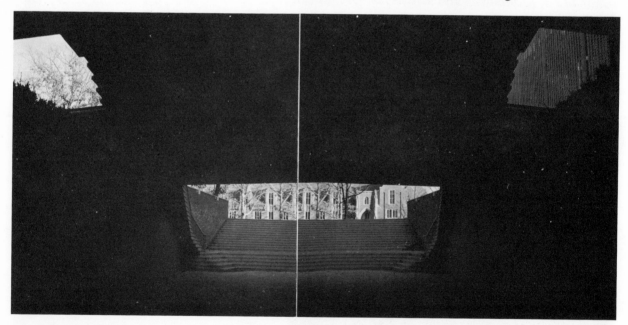

WELLESLEY COLLEGE

A whole new dimension has exploded into view—light coming in high up to left and right. On the left, branches against a blue sky, on the right the enigmatic pattern of the sunbreakers. It is like an electric shock, or drinking a glass of neat bourbon when you expected lemonade. And to let it sink in, there is a long caesura, a halt in the steps. Here, the view at the end resolves itself into being the base of a tower. Then the steps start again, still V-shaped (this is a stroke of absolute genius: they are not just steps, they have become expressive parts of a sequence, and come to the final working out, with the balancing tower and tree full in the view.

36

WELLESLEY COLLEGE

But, even here, there is complication. A second set of steps has come in over our shoulders—with completely different effect from the first, because this set is premised by the arch under which the viewer has passed. To accommodate them there is another short break in the steps, and this by an elementary optical principle is the final "push me–pull you," the exaggeratedly slow gestures before the G-string comes off. Observe.

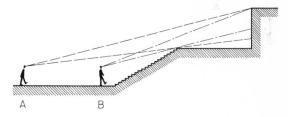

At A one can see half of the tower; at B, nearer the end of the sequence, one can only see the top of it. The trick never fails (and it can be used incidentally in the horizontal plane with a staggered junction. The nearer you get to it, the less you can see).

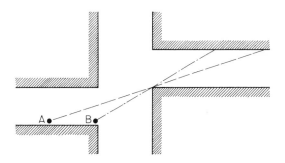

Wellesley has been described in such detail because it is a perfect example of the kind of tools a townscaper needs. These are of the same order as those used in

37

composing a piece of music, and in particular the rhythm of the steps by its unevenness provides the tensions that propel the walker, something quite different from an even pattern. At its simplest, a grid-iron of short and long blocks, wide and narrow streets, is much easier to walk down than a uniform grid. The New Orleans grid is like this (quite apart from the interest and humanity of the buildings). At Wellesley the actual sequence of dimensions, going up, is as follows:

20 PACES	*slight slope*	
3 STEPS		
6 PACES	*flat*	
3 STEPS		
4 PACES	*flat*	(1ST SET OF STAIRS)
3 STEPS		
32 PACES	*flat*	(DIAGONAL UPWARD VIEWS)
5 STEPS		
6 PACES	*flat*	(2ND SET OF STAIRS)
12 STEPS		

There's a good deal more than simple proportion and the golden section here. And there has to be, just as there must be in a human relationship.

The same thing is true of every part of geometry. There is a place for both simple and complex—but there must be *both*, and the simple is really only a special case, though a very important one, among a multitude of complex alternatives. It is the same with curves or gradients. The simplest, bulldozer's way is to do this,

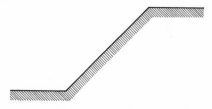

and very effective it can be, when simplicity is needed. But quite a different effect is produced (imagine yourself walking up it) by creating this,

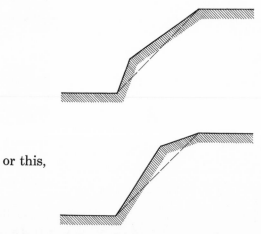

or this,

and an even more subtle, more continuous effect by

this,

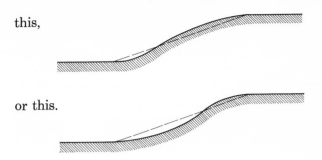

or this.

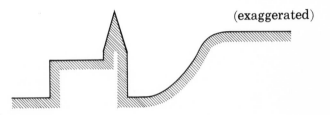

The second of these is actually the shape of New Haven Green; not a straightforward rise up to the front of Yale College, but a double curve, gentle at first, steeper at the end. The famous trio of churches is thus cradled on the green—the miniature

(exaggerated)

spatial theorem has been demonstrated.

Here is another example, serving a direct functional and psychological purpose as well as an aesthetic one. San Clemente, mentioned earlier, is separated from its pier and beach by a railway, in the same way that

SAN CLEMENTE

many American towns are so stupidly cut off from their rivers. The railway must be crossed, and it must be crossed elegantly. People must be led from one side to the other; San Clemente's welfare depends on it, on not being known as the place where the railway blocks off the beach. The use of townscape aesthetics, here

39

(and in many other places and situations), means dollars.

So, here a level crossing cannot be just a level crossing. The simple method

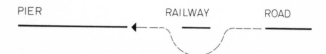

is not enough: it breaks the flow, obtrudes one character on another. But if one goes down and comes up again, the flow is

unimpaired. Does this look ridiculous and further to walk? Perhaps not, if it is done elegantly. Watch how the little conjuring trick is performed. To start with, a tunnel is a degrading thing. You are down, something else is up. Therefore you must be seduced into the tunnel; it must be presented as something which you would go to gratefully, as something of an honor. What is needed is a front, the swish of the matador's cape before the charging bull. And it is provided in defiance of all straight-line logic, by making you go up before you go down.

Here it is in fact,

SAN CLEMENTE

and the artists in town making have done their job well. You are made to want to go up to the little belvedere with its seats. You are even helped, close to, by the brick steps, steps which make you part of the environment by being gently worn.

40

SAN CLEMENTE

Towns only become truly themselves when they have been used for some time—a Kleenex town center which is thrown away every few years is quite practicable: it is just that it ignores all the human desires for warmth and growth and permanence—i.e., that in fundamental terms it is insanely incomplete. In other words, in any real sense it is impracticable also.

Once on the belvedere, this open-air lesson in psychology shows its hand.

SAN CLEMENTE

You see the goal—shipshape and elegant in a way that very few instruments of pleasure in America are. You see the obstacle also, but by the simple expedient of **41** rising a few feet, you see over it and beyond it. To

cross it by a tunnel now becomes, what it would not
have been before, an act of accommodation, not an
imposition forced on you. It becomes a pleasure. So
down you go

and under

SAN CLEMENTE

When you look back,

SAN CLEMENTE

you wonder how on earth the transition was achieved. It was achieved by the exercise of townscape and its effect is to make an enjoyment out of necessity. It can do the same for every street in America.

But to be able to do so townscape must have continuous space—the point made in the last chapter. One thing must lead to the next. This means that there must be found some form of cracking the gridiron, and a later chapter will try to explore a few of the possibilities: the great hope is not so much the alteration of the street plan but the use of the third dimension, up and down, and the creation of a pedestrian's city superimposed on the grid to make a completely different pattern: two cities existing on the same piece of ground.

It also means, rather more simply, that the space cannot have leaks. If there is a gap, it must mean something: otherwise the sequence and the experience

43

break down. The town full of meaningless holes is as useless, in this sense, as a raincoat in the same condition. And now take a look at San Antonio. Carmel, New York, or Sandusky, Ohio,

SAN ANTONIO

CARMEL

CARMEL

or even part of one of the Savannah squares.

In each case any kind of meaningful pattern is made impossible by leaks in the space, either through parking lots or because of too low and too flimsy buildings. It can happen if the road is too wide even though the buildings around are tall and solid—this view of the main square of Youngstown, Ohio, shows the effect of

a decent central square—the only meaningful space that Youngstown has—invalidated by the exit being too wide. There's nothing there; space is galloping off up the road. Containment, the sense of space, of a "here" as opposed to a different "there," has gone. It can happen on a larger scale by the completely chaotic high skyline which is the *chef-d'oeuvre* of many American cities. Because of it, Rittenhouse Square in Philadelphia, for all its leafiness, has so much pointless and formless variety to the buildings around it (from four to forty stories) that it ceases

45

to read as a square at all. It has become a pedestrian traffic circle: you can never feel happy in it. Its twin, Washington Square behind Independence Hall, is

RITTENHOUSE SQUARE

quite different. There the buildings are about the same height, the enclosure is preserved, the square remains

WASHINGTON SQUARE

a square. There may be less light and fewer trees, but it remains more of an oasis. (In passing, this problem is quite different from that posed by the famous views of the New York skyline from Central Park. In that, each part of each view has established its identity, there is no question of one destroying another. Instead, widely differing identities meet, and enhance each other by contrast.)

In all these cases the objection is not to parking lots, gas stations, etc., as such. They can be organized in many different ways to enhance the sense of place instead of destroying it. (For just one example: as a ring right around the downtown center, thickly planted with trees, some form of green lung and parking lot in one.) The choice is quite simple. If these objects are scattered broadcast through the city center, then the chances of making a coherent townscape that is more than a set of clever snippets are negligible. It is like making bricks without straw, and the point is not moral but optical—though, goddamit, the center of a town is for people, not for their empty, outsize, metallic raincoats.

The difference between sequences in different places is a very large part of identity. So the next sequence discussed is a very simple one that, as its subject is a small place, completely defines its identity. It also, incidentally, makes two other points. One is that identity is something which is not at all a special case, unlike San Clemente or Wellesley College: it could happen in almost any small town in America. And the other is that it is, I am sure, quite unrecognized. Little towns, particularly courthouse towns, have a great deal of individuality waiting to be discovered; and the realization need not be a costly business.

This particular courthouse town is in Hillsboro, Illinois, not far from St. Louis. It depends as usual on a variation in the grid, though a slight one: simply that the road leading up to the courthouse has a kink in it. Not

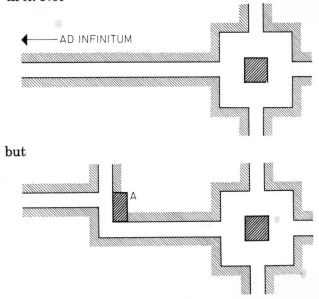

but

The view is articulated, not endless. Hillsboro is given a signature tune. It is lucky, because the building A is a pleasant one, an eye-catcher.

HILLSBORO Behind it the courthouse itself, in its jolly (and under-
rated) 1870 dress, just comes into view, like a child
appearing behind Aunt Matilda. Immediately, a relationship and a tension, a little lesson in perspective.
It is a come-on: you want to go round the corner and
see this thing close up. When you do,

The courthouse, already apprehended as a whole, is
continually having a fan dance performed in front of
it by the overhanging signs. This is admirable, and
there is a double counterpoint, both visual and intellectual, in the confrontation of "Maymie's Café"
and "Montgomery County Loans" with the august
symbol of county justice in the background. In the
countryside these signs would be (and are) abortions,
caused by the meeting of incompatible strains. In a
town street they are in their natural place, and to
suggest removing them, as the people of Kalamazoo
want to do in their pedestrian mall, is perhaps natural,
but would be disastrous: a confusion between tidying
up a town and preserving its character. They are not
necessarily the same thing at all. Some parts may
need tidyness, some may thrive on chaos: as in life,
there is no one law for everything. Some buildings may
need symmetry; some, like the Hillsboro courthouse
with which this chapter takes its leave, get on very
well with the highly incorrect apposition of a mansard
roof and a cornice.

48

HILLSBORO it is the typical courthouse main street; but it can be varied—as most such streets can be varied—by an observant trip up the sidewalk. The visual consequences are clear in these two views.

HILLSBORO

4 | IDENTITY

My most memorable day in America was not in Vermont or Arizona. It was a long westward journey through the Panhandle of Oklahoma and northwest Texas, and it was made memorable because of the fact that—almost alone in the U.S.A.—each tiny town had identity of the most breathtaking and sublime sort. The distance ceased to be so many miles, and became a delightful progression from one piece of nobility to the next. The agents of the nobility were the grain elevators; and though not every town in America possesses such unconscious masterpieces, so much better than the usual labored-over "Fine Arts Center," the lessons they have to teach are universal.

I started out from Seiling, west of Enid, at eight o'clock on a December morning, bright and crystal clear. On top of the first rise, with the desperate evidences of the Big Blow all around, something white glinted on the horizon twenty miles away. With every hilltop of the loping, rolling road the glint persisted, like a star. At last the scale and monotony of America began to make sense, was stressed, had a point to it, instead of being just so many degrees of latitude and longitude and nothing else.

The star expanded, took on form, took on a counterpoint of forms, and at last, in the little village of Vici, with a population of six hundred and twenty, was the answer to the problem I had been looking for all the way across America—a place that was all identity, that could be nowhere else, expressed through its physical shape.

It is here simply a matter of a unique conformation of objects—a relationship—but watch the subtlety provided from the moment, a mile out, when the camera can pick up the skyline, though the eye has had it in view for half an hour.

VICI

Here are other things also: the admirably direct road numbering, conveying its information in terms of the landscape, in signs and shapes, not words; and then the relationship set up between this pair of objects, sign and elevator, one epitomizing flow, the other epitomizing a static place. Not just road and village, unaccented, but Road expressed and Village expressed —contrasted opposites, not an average; hence, variety and identity, not monotony.

This is not just any old contrast, but a selected,* controlled contrast, with the important things, the essences, kept important in the view (if you have a good figure you dress to accentuate it). A few yards away along the road is the other thing, the any-old-contrast, with the glorious crystalline shapes almost obscured by the ads for cars and gasoline. It is not the billboard that is wrong but its positioning and relationship.

VICI   (BILLBOARD)

Another few yards, and the Rolleiflex has constructed another little theorem of excitement. More counterpoint between flow and stop, this time with railways and telegraph lines: now, also, counterpoint in the forms of the elevators and sheds themselves.

VICI   (RAILROAD)

These take over, play the sublime game, black against white, cylindrical against angular,

VICI

* I know it is accidental, here. I had to do the selection and controlling by Rolleiflex: it should have been in the landscape by design.

until the big silos seem to overpower the whole view

VICI

and the smaller sheds have their even smaller counter-point,

VICI

while the humbler checkerboard of streets intensifies the effect by its domesticity.

VICI

52

This is, it really is, like having a Michelangelo in the backyard—or like having the whole backyard made into a Michelangelo. And for a stretch in the Panhandle of Texas, every town's backyard is a different masterpiece. At Dumas, it is a pair, subtly different, among the rail tracks;

DUMAS

at Hartley, it is simply one enormous silo beside the road in a place with hardly a dozen houses to it.

HARTLEY

53

All this is accident—the same kind of accident that produced Cotswold stone cottages or the shapes of Vermont barns. Without the accident, Vici and Dumas and Hartley would be like ten thousand other American communities: with it, the job is only half done. It needs to be exploited, as Venice exploited what was to begin with just a set of marshy islands in a lagoon. These silos are far and away the biggest things there: the urban center could congregate round them—if it wanted to—like a Flemish Grand-Place, in a couple of irregular squares, taking advantage of the sunny or shady sides according to season, vast awnings stretched from the silo sides, open market (or supermarket: there's no need to import Europeanisms if they are not welcome), each square different, each town with a different shape coming quite naturally from the different layout of the silos.

Identity, in this physical, townscape sense, is a unique configuration of all the objects that go to make up the town, natural and man-made. The town planner's or townscaper's job is to recognize and exploit the potentialities of each particular site, express them in a unique way, and in a way which matches the emotional and human needs of the inhabitants. Stuyvesant Town in New York City is, undoubtedly, a physical identity, but the price paid for it in human terms is far too great. Levittown is some sort of a solution for some human needs, but has no physical identity (and hence, in the end, will fail in the deeper human terms too). The problem is to balance and harmonize: heart and head acting together.

Sometimes, in small places, one simple gesture is enough. In Europe it is usually the informal relationship of church and village, sometimes the more calculated, formal bow of a tiny regular plan, completely successful because it can be seen to have limits. Many European and almost all American regular plans go on far too long, and hence lose their effect completely—in this case too much of a good thing is not only a surfeit, it changes character completely—servant becomes master. But in a few tiny places the exquisite elegance of a formal gesture of the right shape and size still exists and makes them unforgettable. One of these is Newfane, a tiny courthouse village northwest of Brattleboro in Vermont.

NEWFANE

Another, ghostly now, is the fragment of the piazza Bertram Goodhue built in Tyrone, New Mexico, for a mining town which was never finished.
Here, the county jail is on one side of the road, across a square green, and three public buildings are on the other—the Courthouse, the Church, and the Union Hall, all backed by a wooded hill. They are as symmetrically arranged as the partners in a minuet, each with its spire, but—this is an important thing—each is as different in detail as the faces and figures of the dancing partners would be. Asymmetry-in-symmetry, a tension and a subtlety that is so much more than

54

TYRONE

complete regularity, just as ⌐ is so much more than ⌐ This, actually, is part of the answer to resolving the dialectic between individual freedom and a planned environment. Each can be provided where the need is greatest if it is prepared to give way to the other elsewhere. If neither gives in anywhere, then both perish, destroying one another—the commuter's car journey into town has no order and no individual freedom either. The gridiron city has no freedom and no order worth respecting either.

Not every place has three Colonial steeples to play with: the point is taken. But nearly every place has some kind of shape to use as a starting point; here is a selection of objects of more general application. If the object makes some kind of spiritual sense, so much the better: important objects ought to serve an important purpose, and this really is the basic fallacy of the outsize billboard, that what is being advertised is not important. But "spiritual" objects have a much wider range than the overtly religious. For example, a water tower at Pensacola beach in Florida;

PENSACOLA BEACH

55

another kind of grain elevator from Windsor near Mattoon in Illinois;

WINDSOR

a factory at Litchfield near St. Louis;

LITCHFIELD

a drive-in cinema—a completely neglected source of visual focus and excitement—in Texas;

NEAR FORT WORTH

56

Decatur has its missed opportunity, the fallow land between shops and rail tracks, which is waste ground or a parking lot.

Here, as in so many American towns, the space for a true gesture of identity and urbanity is ready-made. It could be a small square, a courtyard, part of an arch over the road, anything: it is just waiting to be used, thus

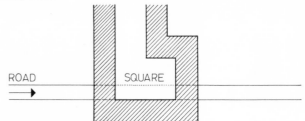

or this

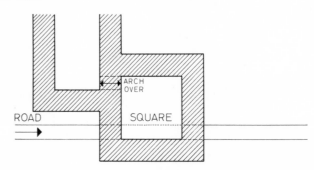

The combinations are endless.

The other example is even simpler and cruder, to show that no place, however tiny or accidental, has absolutely nothing in it which cannot be seized on and adapted. Wellton, Arizona, is a tiny place between Yuma and Phoenix on US 80, in desert that is just beginning to be irrigated and cultivated, a yellow flat between orange mountains. The population is three hundred: one church, one tiny hotel, diners, a couple of banks, a school—

60

apart from the backdrop it could be a thousand places on a thousand state roads. Yet its potentiality is there, as faint as a charcoal smudge. The old street of houses —thirty years old, maybe?—has been by-passed by US 80, which sweeps to one side.

Banks and gas stations and diners are arranged around US 80 into a new equivalent of the Grand-Place or the Western street wide enough to turn an ox-team in.

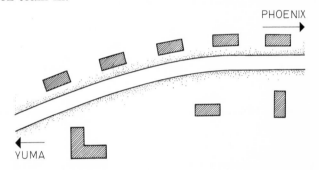

So here, right away, is the potential contrast between the domestic grid and the new-style "market place," which only needs accentuating—links between the buildings, new buildings carefully placed to accentuate the contrast and define the shape, to look a little like this:

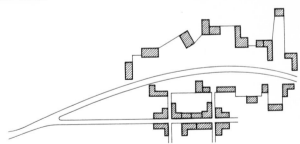

This could take one of a hundred forms: once the pattern is recognized then the details can be completely free. Views out of the "market place" could be angled on the mountains which are superb, on midsummer or midwinter sunrises and sunsets, as relevant today as they ever were in the time of the Indians. Anything is possible, and in America more than any other country in the world, at any time. You have only to will it and want it enough.

Although Wellton is sited in spectacular landscape, natural site plays no essential part in this little theorem of identity. In most American cities it cannot, now, because the battle is already lost—it is a terrible

61

loss, too—for once our artifacts have flowed further than the eye can see, they might as well go on undifferentiated as far as Fairbanks, Alaska. It is little use that Boston and its suburbs are built around an exciting set of estuaries when the mid-twentieth century simply steamrollers over the whole landscape as stupidly as the nineteenth-century builders did when they filled in the Back Bay and made an ordinary metropolitan city out of one of the most emotive situations in the world. The point is not necessarily that the Back Bay should not have been filled in, but that whatever was done should have been done imaginatively. The first sight of outer Boston in the early morning from the transatlantic airplane into New York is one of the saddest introductions to any country, just as the sea approach to Manhattan is one of the most exhilarating.

But, in a few particular cases and one general case, the riverside site has been too much for even the cruellest misuse. The general case is that nobody has yet found a way to build subdivisions on water on a commercial scale so that rivers stay rivers and there is still the basic contrast of liquid vs. solid. That I want to return to. The handful of particular cases are well known and become an attraction, something to go and see, precisely because of this. The best refutation of the fact that people enjoy eternal monotony is that they are always chasing after something different, whether a new country or a new woman. Hence, in their different ways, the waterfronts of Manhattan, Pittsburgh, San Francisco, and New Orleans. There aren't very many more examples of this inner logic. One of them, in its quiet way, is Tallahassee, where ridgetop siting has given an exquisite logic to the shape of the town, quite accidental and largely unrealized, running south along the ridge from US 90 through the commercial gridiron to the domed state capitol, with mostly countryside beyond and in the valleys on either side of the ridge.

But probably the best of all, potentially, is Madison, Wisconsin. Goop flows around Madison for ten miles or more, and the fact that the 9999th house may have been designed by Frank Lloyd Wright is, when you get there, utterly irrelevant. But the situation of the center is fantastic, as a glance at the map will show— an isthmus of land separating two large lakes, with the commercial heart and the state capitol bang in the middle, on a small hill. Even the visitor hardened to disappointments (for the *map* of America is one of the most exciting in the world), such as the actual looks of Cleveland, Boston, Baton Rouge, thinks that this time some of the opportunity must have been realized. So it has, and the first view of Madison across Lake Monona is a catharsis, like the first view of Chartres or Venice. But it is not realized close to, unlike Chartres or Venice, although it could be quite easily.

MADISON   **62**

The way in which Madison could be realized shows exactly how sites and buildings interact to give different identities and how these can be enhanced and differentiated instead of being overlaid or ignored. The lake-to-lake section through the state capitol is very roughly like this:

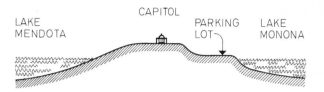

This means that the two sides of the isthmus have utterly different physical characters and have developed different man-made characters. The Mendota shore is quiet and domestic, lawns and seats and a good small parking lot showing that it is not cars themselves that are bad things but what is done with them: if they are brought into relationship with the view instead of obliterating it, they can be a landscape asset. Here the means are very simple—tree trunks as barriers, freedom from pointless signs, someone to pick up the trash.

MADISON

The other side is more dramatic, more exciting but less realized. What happens is a really admirable short, formal axis leading from the capitol to the end of the bluff: the right length, the right size, and something worth while at the other end, not just an endless gallop out into the prairie.

63

MADISON

MADISON

Then, finally, at the bluff edge with the lake tempting, appealing, beckoning on, there is a crashing, grinding full stop: no way down, and the lakeside chock-full of cars—here blurring and obliterating, not part of the scene.

MADISON

It is a slap across the face with a cold, wet fish, one of the cruelest disappointments in America. Yet it could so easily be transformed—no cars in the space on line with the axis, boating stages and a splendid Spanish Steps effect (please, not carried out in Beaux-Arts Renaissance stonework—there's no point in putting on funny hats), scissoring down the wall (arrowed on the photograph) to the lakeside, or

MADISON

reaching right over the road and railway to the edge of the lake itself. This is the case of townscape potential shouting so loud that it almost deafens you.

The Madison waterfront could in fact be like the Savannah waterfront, a wonderfully rich multilevel piece of townscape which is as remarkable as the Savannah squares: an expressway landscape two hundred years old but without any of the contempt for two-legged animals implied in an expressway interchange. This is a living, working part of a real town, not an abstract theorem about ants. The situation is almost exactly like the Monona side of Madison, i.e., a bluff and a foreshore. The warehouses and offices

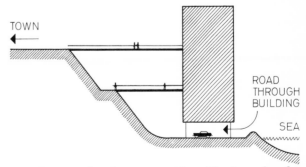

TOWN

ROAD THROUGH BUILDING

SEA

are built at the bottom end with two levels of pedestrian access bridging what appears to be the ravine, with roads winding down to the quayside

through the buildings. The whole thing is put together

like a watch, and put together with all kinds of humane touches. It has a magnificent identity, something that is purely Savannah. It is also quite unselfconscious, and this is the final refinement that the conscious townscaper, an *uomo universale* if ever one was needed, has to apply—to know when to stop, to know when accident ought to take over in the pattern. In some cases things can be left to chance, in others everything needs to be detailed, down to the bollards. Every place is different.

With Savannah, once the pattern has been set, then everything inside it is almost bound to enhance the richness. (Examples of what wouldn't: a parking lot, a fussy public park, a gap doing nothing, a smoothing down of the gradient.) It is built up of two things—the different levels, so that three or four different kinds of bustle are going on in the same space, and the humane details, as unusual in America (and, in the end, as necessary to any comprehensive form of civilized urban life) as a courteous traffic cop. Trees, delicate but not whimsical handrails, a pattern of setts in the road, are all tiny recognitions that man is a partner in his environment. They have a townscape job, to articulate and inflect; they also have a much more generalized importance which is as immediate and relevant as the genuine smile in a shop, the friendly handshake.

HUMANE DETAILS

But, for one Savannah there are a hundred squalid, pointless turnings-away from American rivers. The hatred is almost pathological—the standard pattern of neglected banks, railroad yards, fag-ends of town pulling away their skirts from the too-too nasty mess. A whole book could be written on American river

MULTI-LEVEL

banks alone, for they form the biggest single waste of opportunity in the whole environment. And not only rivers—some places (fishing and tourist places, even) actually manage to turn their backs on the *sea*. Just how disintegrated can urban life get? Gulfport is like this; a good beach, a fine busy little harbor, vitality and bustle building up very well. Intricacy of function and complexity of shape and plan going on hand in hand, as it always should. It is a Fisherman's Wharf in Mississippi, if people only had eyes to see it. But then, behind it, bang (or rather, whimper), nearly a mile of nothing, with the town center genteelly self-contained at the other end of it.

GULFPORT FROM GULFPORT BEACH

This results in the whole *raison d'etre* of the place being neglected and isolated. The town should be growing out of its beach and harbor naturally. Even if the buildings of present-day Gulfport were the most elegant in the world, the total effect would still be unhappy and fragmented. As in so many American towns, the damage is not irreparable, but Gulfport must understand its patterns. *Laissez faire* will never do it, now. Form and pattern no longer follow function automatically: but the point of their doing so is still as strong as ever.

Gulfport is an extreme case, but there are hundreds of others: towns all down the Mississippi which are cut off from the river by the railway—something which can be remedied without necessarily scrapping the railway. The other side of the tracks never had a sadder meaning than the superb, wasted landscape and townscape of American riversides. Cassville, Dubuque, Savanna, Clinton, and Rock Island were the ones I saw, a whole roll call of missed opportunity. It might sound impossible for an island site in the middle of the Mississippi, one of the world's great rivers in spirit as well as size, to be utterly drab and characterless, but Rock Island achieves it. At the other end of the river Baton Rouge is separated from its levees by rail tracks and a block of slums—levees which ought to be the landscape focus of the whole city. Brattleboro in Vermont has a wonderful foaming confluence of the Connecticut and a small river right in the middle of town—yet there is almost no place from which it is even visible, and then all that is to be seen is a mess of scrub, trash, electricity substations. It is like marrying a beautiful wife and then bundling her up until only the nose and elbows show.

Even St. Louis, which has its whole life and history tied to the river banks, develops as a pattern only for a hundred yards or so—a magnificent Mississippi-scale pattern with a broad sweep of setts running up from the steamers so that the parked cars are tamed

ST. LOUIS

and brought into the pattern by being seen on the slope. But then the whole thing disintegrates into a waste land, and there is no continuity between river and city. This will alter, soon, when the Jefferson Memorial Arch is built—but unless the planners are very sensitive it will merely replace one waste land by another. There must be life pulsing and flowing all the way from the city center to the river edge: if the Memorial Arch establishes one great green axis up to the courthouse, then that is enough: on either side there should be a mixture of as many different uses as can be made to lie down together. Chicago's lakeside is surely the proof of that: the vast uninhabited sweep of parking lot and gardens does not unite city and lake but separates them irrevocably; to get from Michigan Avenue to the shore requires a real effort of will, instead of being easy, inviting, seductive.

Obviously, not every riverside should be a bustling, working one: it depends on the specific character of the place; and if the meeting of town and river is almost accidental, as it often is in America, there is no point in forcing a shotgun marriage. Then the river

69

becomes the quiet, contemplative part of the town, rather than its center of vitality: the point is that it must be *something*. If the riverside is to be landscape rather than townscape, it must be done sensitively yet firmly, and above all without fuss or whimsy, keeping the rhythm as large-scale and smooth-flowing as the river itself. The answer is not this—Chicago again—

CHICAGO LAKESIDE with a mass of formal geometry, cars all over the place and nothing still or harmonious, but this,

WILKES-BARRE

WILKES-BARRE

a treatment so elegant and large-scale and sympathetic that it comes over clearly even in the gray November light in which these pictures were taken. They come from Wilkes-Barre, the river is the Susquehanna. By simply making a terrace on the river bank and cutting an arch through the bridge abutment, a linear walk is created which is insulated from cars yet always only a few yards from the town center. And none of the details

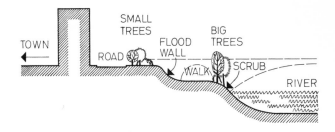

let down the total conception, which is the final hallmark of a masterpiece: the planting of big and small trees where each is needed, the simple handrail echoing the riverside line, the path left grassy, not concreted over or adorned with notices. But for every Wilkes-Barre, how many hundreds of Rock Islands are there?

71

5 | LIMITS AND CONTRAST, UNITY-IN-DIVERSITY

In the last chapter, Newfane in Vermont could fairly be called a single identity: there is just one single outdoor space or arrangement of objects. But all of the other examples are more complex. In some cases, like the site of Pittsburgh, there is a controlling idea on the largest scale inside which the dozens of separate identities of the city can be self-expressive; in others, such as Savannah, the riverside is one distinct identity which comes up against the other overriding identity of the town—the repeating pattern of squares—and makes up the total place additively. In other words, the identity of any sizable place is likely to be the sum of all kinds of smaller identities, with, in all the best examples, probably one or two larger threads drawing them together. In Midtown Manhattan, all of the avenues and most of the streets have quite distinct identities, pulled together by the sense of the East and Hudson rivers at the ends of each cross-city view (a sense which is not quite realized physically. Everyone knows, intellectually, the shape of Manhattan, but it cannot be sensed visually at, say, the corner of Eighth Avenue and Fiftieth Street. Some kind of come-on is needed, the sort provided by the ships' funnels at the end of Canal Street in New Orleans. It could even be done with reflectors high up, to give the glint of water).

So each place is a collection of identities—whether the place is a village, a town, or a whole countryside. This is, I think, the only key to sorting out the American environment as a whole, and this point will be taken further later. At the moment the point is to explore what happens at the edges of these identities, and to see how they interact.

The first essential is that the place or identity must have clear limits. If you have on successive courses two plates (a T-bone steak and apple pie, say) and allow their edges to mix, then the sense of identity of either, and contrast between the two, disappears; and the transition, the period when you are eating T-bone pie or apple steak, is remarkably horrible although both may be very good in themselves. This may sound a simple proposition but it takes the townscaper into deep water. For the entire perimeter of every American town is a vast T-bone apple pie; town and country or suburb and country mixed and diluted horribly and almost irretrievably—a confusion of identities.

That is on the biggest scale, but the same thing is true of all smaller identities. In each distinct part of the town you ought to be able to feel "I am in it," "I am near the edge of it," "I am just outside it." So that the town is a collection of distinct areas, not an amorphous gray mass—just as the members of a family must exist as individuals, not stereotypes. This analogy is exact. Traveling by train from Philadelphia to Chicago there was a family party of about eight bound for a wedding in Beaver Falls, which is just beyond Pittsburgh. They colonized one end of the car and through that long, cold Pennsylvania night with conductors on snowy platforms calling out names like Altoona and Johnstown as a marine sergeant might wake up a barrack room, they constructed an ideal town for a few hours just as tangibly as though it were bricks and mortar. One woman was the dynamo for the whole party—equivalent to the overriding pattern of Pittsburgh or San Francisco, if you like—but she acted as a dynamo, not a steam roller: she vitalized the other members so that each contributed to the whole themselves, the noisy ones and the quiet ones both, a perfect miniature of a city made up of separate identities, each distinct and definite. If each had been less themselves, the whole thing would have sagged—and so with cities.

The particular townscape problem is to recognize identities and then to give them visual limits, or identify their limits with visual punctuation or articulation. The simplest definition of all is the town wall, something which may seem ridiculously out of place in a book on twentieth-century America. Yet one of the most famous American institutions is exactly that—the Chicago Loop. Being inside the Loop is both an emotional and functional identity, made immediately into a physical identity by a look along any street. At any crossroads the whole thing is as elegantly manifest as in a French bastide town or an Italian Renaissance fortress. The means by which this effect is achieved in Chicago may be unnecessarily man-hating, for almost all American cities are too uniformly hard, just as some European cities are too soft—

CHICAGO LOOP

but the rightness of the effect is unmistakable. The streets which have the Loop going down the middle of them, like Wabash, are, incidentally, naturals for covering with awnings, thereby making them into pedestrian malls and markets (see p. 142).

With this loop-identity created and recognized, the area outside it should have been treated quite differently, to accentuate the loop-ness of the Loop. Instead, it remains no more than a fortunate man-made accident.

Other clear man-made visual limits are hard to find in America. One of the best is at Wilkes-Barre where the memorial bridge over the Susquehanna has a pair of triumphant arches which act exactly like city gates, indicating the edge of town from half a mile away,

WILKES-BARRE

and for which we have to thank the eclectic talents of Carrère and Hastings. On a much smaller scale a tiny place like Springer in New Mexico has a railway arch at its southern end which quite accidentally marks the end of present building. It ought to mark the end of future building too, in this case, and keep the division between town and country sharp and exciting. And a single street can do it, perhaps too self-consciously, like this:

MAIDEN LANE

It all helps definition, the recognition of boundaries, of insides and outsides of places, of "Here" and "There."

The easiest means of definition is by vertical separation, and this is the basis of any workable coexistence between pedestrian and automobile on a large scale— and also the easiest and simplest way of breaking down the geometrical tyranny of the gridiron. What is needed is separation, not necessarily segregation. As little as three feet up or down can transport the pedestrian into another identity entirely. At Charleston, a waterfront path becomes a different place by raising it seven steps above the road,

CHARLESTON

and here the difference is largely a simple psychological thing, that of looking down on the roofs of cars. Mellon Square in Pittsburgh does the same thing on a larger scale. But an equivalent separation down can have the same effect—the Midway Gardens in Chicago are about three feet below the street level,

MIDWAY GARDENS

and immediately it is a different place, utterly different from the effect of the same area of grass at street level—and incidentally having the splendid property of being able to be flooded in winter and then used as an ice rink. Here again, as at Wilkes-Barre, the landscape is on a splendid scale, nothing fussy or messy—the steps are real man-size Chicago steps,

MIDWAY GARDENS

without being in the least inhuman.

Another way of defining things is the way that the bull defines the red rag—by meeting it head-on, without mediation. It is the opposite of the fenced-off or behind-bars attitudes to life—opposites come together sharply and vitalize the contrast thereby. Three examples of this trick, which can be called immediacy, will indicate the range; it is not, of course, like anything else in this book, a universal solution, but one to be applied with discrimination, perpetually adjusting the idea to particular cases. In Brunswick, Georgia, that endearing kid brother of Savannah, it is the effect of a tree in the middle of the street, without railings or notices or flower beds.

BRUNSWICK

NEW YORK

In a much-better-known example, it is the sudden apocalyptic view you get on stepping out of the elevator on top of Rockefeller Center—no corridors, no halfway views, the whole lot at once.

77

78 And in the stricter sense of the contrast of different identities it is this ship's bow jutting directly over the street of one of the Navy berths on the Delaware at Philadelphia. The same ship seen behind a high wall would not be nearly so effective.

PHILADELPHIA

Another aspect of identities which starts by being a common sense extension of definitions and ends up by being a most powerful townscape instrument is the idea of different kinds of identity. Obviously there are as many different identities of place as there are of people. Some can be grouped roughly, as people can, into easily recognizable patterns—city center, farmland, mountainous desert, leafy suburb. But there are many more, and the twentieth century is creating them every day (or rather, providing the raw materials for the townscaper to create them). This is or could so easily be the positive side of the technological explosion, for never have so many weird and exciting objects been poured out on the landscape. They need to be poured out with discrimination and arranged with art, and if you think after reading this far that I mean airy-fairy, you're in the wrong book. For example, *this* is an identity, with its own internal laws,

SAN DIEGO OIL FIELD

and so is this,

SAFFORD SUBSTATION

just as much as this, which is a few miles further on (near Safford, Arizona, on US 70).

MOUNTAINS

And equally, so is this (Safford, again).

SAFFORD AGAIN

As long as roadtown does not happen in every street— a point that is made evident in an unobtrusive way in Safford, for the main street ending in the courthouse is a block away from US 70 and has a quieter, quite different character. The important thing is to recognize the multitude of different identities, and allow them all to work out their own terms.

This idea has, I think, never been consciously and consistently applied in essence, but a pallid ghost of it is one of the town planner's stock-in-trades, in the shape of zoning. That ghost must be laid, here and now: to practice use-zoning and imagine that you are thereby practicing the art of defining identities is as much of a delusion as swallowing the right vitamin pills in the right order and imagining that you are enjoying a banquet. Some germ of use-zoning is in the idea of identity, as the vitamins are in the pheasant and the pâté, but only as a tiny part, not an overriding, regulating thing. Identity is organic, a mixture of all life's influences, not something to be treated in chopped-up bits called home, work, recreation. This may take some grasping, because on the face of it the whole idea of identities could be called a chopping-up of continuous existence. The difference is between isolating a complex molecule or cell, something which is an exact microcosm of the larger self—equivalent to identity—and splitting up the atom into separate electrons and protons, changing its character and essence completely and sometimes producing an explosion—which, all too often, is what is achieved by use-zoning. If you begin to get the feeling that this is an emotional and complex matter, needing as much care as a mature relationship, then you are exactly right. This book could consist of several hundred "rules," all of which would probably improve things in most cases for most of the time—but this would be quite pointless, because what is needed is a new way of thinking.

Here are two rough examples, fragments of sorting out into identities, made after a few minutes' observation in either case. They may thus be an incorrect diagnosis, but they do not vitiate the principle. In Louisville, Kentucky, the main square is divided into two by a link between City Hall and its extension.

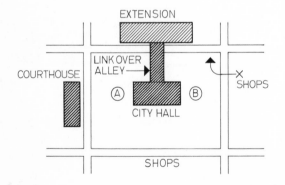

LOUISVILLE

It is almost nothing, yet it demarcates quite clearly two identities, A being purely civic, B being civic, social and commercial. The street corner at X, for example, just happens to be the one where casual semi-official conversations go on; to recognize it, the good townscaper needs the sensitiveness of a novelist as well as a painter. A and B ought to be heightened in their different ways, even to the point of separating them physically in front of the city hall as well as behind it. Every county seat has a courthouse square: but a pair of them, each related but with its own character, would be something very different.

The second example, much less circumstantial, comes from Pensacola. A good deal of modern Pensacola is characterlessness at its worst, but it is one of the oldest places in America, and before it exploded a very definite pattern grew up, helped by the topography, which could easily today be recovered with a little care. Much of the trouble here, as almost everywhere else in the U. S. A., is that nadir of self-respect, the vacant lot; it would be no infringement of individual liberty if municipal government could find the legal formula necessary to be able to say to the owners —to adapt a phrase—put up or sell up: either build or sell to somebody else who will.

The natural axis of Pensacola is Main Street, running North-South and ending on the shore in "made land," an artificial spit of rock from all over the world brought to the town in ballast by the ships which **PENSACOLA** exported timber.

This street is naturally commercial and industrial—no need to be rigid about it—but is gap-toothed especially at the south end and needs building up and intensifying. At the moment it is like a backbone with some vertebrae missing. Running parallel with it is Pensacola's backside of car lots and railway tracks, which is quite different from the front and a natural for making into a tree-lined boulevard or a linear park (the cars could still stay under the trees, as they do in many European squares). Immediately beyond is Seville Square, still leafy, quiet, and charmingly domestic, though it needs a careful watch kept on it.

PENSACOLA

So here within a few yards there are potentially three quite different identities, which, fitting together, thanks to Pensacola Bay, make a pattern which could be one of the sights of America; for, in addition to all this, there is the coastline too.

82

PENSACOLA

PENSACOLA

And every town has the same things waiting to be discovered and exploited. It would be an absorbing project for either university or municipality to sort out just one ordinary-sized American town into identities, and to try to accentuate the "is-ness" of each part. There is the point, already made, of wide divergence and the excitement to be got from establishing the contrasts; there is also the subtler pleasure of unity-in-diversity, of the repeating pattern which is slightly different in each case, and the added excitement of going through this pattern in sequence, with the memory of the other identity (square, park, street) counterpointing the present experience. I suppose it must be like making love to twin sisters. The grid can be of use here, and this effect can be got quite accidentally in midtown Manhattan by walking up, say, Seventh Avenue around Fortieth Street: each cross street seems to house a different trade and cross-**83** section of people. More formally it can be given by

TEXAS COURTHOUSES

the pattern of courthouse squares seen in a cross-country journey—these four come from US 180 west of Fort Worth.

The supreme American example is the glorious plan of Savannah, where each street developed a chain of squares as it went back from the waterfront. A walk here is not just so many blocks, but a living sequence—each square doing a different job, and giving a different punctuation.

Starting with Johnson Square and its obelisk,

SAVANNAH

SAVANNAH

SAVANNAH

the path continues across the road—its priority clearly indicated by lines (an essential, here)—to a very similar square. Yet in the middle, no obelisk but the extraordinary Van Brunt Gordon memorial, a splendid object to have in a town. From here, again, the next square beckons: but what beckons far more is the steeple of Independence Church, off axis.

SAVANNAH

85

This appears to be in the next square, but in fact is on the corner of a cross-street, Oglethorpe Avenue, full of trees and full of benches.

SAVANNAH

SAVANNAH

The urban texture has become as intricate and delicate as a Haydn quartet or a good jazz quartet: there are no brows in this business. Beyond, the next square, Chippewa, is actually ushered in by the church school with a pediment of the same dimensions as Independence Church, but attached to a completely different building. Again, another expression of unity-in-diversity.

86

SAVANNAH

SAVANNAH

The walk goes on through three more squares and ends among squirrels and pigeons at a gleaming white fountain in Forsyth Park, which is so big that the houses around the sides are barely visible. Beyond

SAVANNAH

here was open country—and could be again, if when rebuilding America dared to create opposites, i.e., a tongue of park or farmland running right into the city as the counterpoint of the city's expansion into the country.

There is only one Savannah in America, though there is no reason at all why a plan of equal scale and humanity should not be part of every new urban renewal scheme. But this trick of unity-in-diversity can be done much more simply. The simplest way of all is with trees. Trees are not just a vegetable amenity: they are living partners in the environment, they can do as many different things if they are used imaginatively as the different ways there are of saying "Hi." Sometimes there are four or five different uses in one place, like this sequence from Union Square, San Francisco.

UNION SQUARE

UNION SQUARE

And here is another set of trees doing different things. Statistically they are all just trees. In the same way, to far too many architects and planners, people to be rehoused in urban renewal projects are just so many heads. But look at trees individually and this is what they can do: act as a punctuation mark, a lift of the eyebrows, to give scale to buildings—

SAVANNAH

the opposite of this is to fan dance in front of a building, to make more attractive and mysterious by concealment; the technique is familiar,

PHILADELPHIA CHURCH

—fill a gap in a street reassuringly bushily,

NEW ORLEANS

—or with exquisite tendril tenderness,

NEW ORLEANS

—act as a focal point; even the artificiality of a Christmas tree makes all the difference to this little square in Somerset, Pennsylvania,

SOMERSET

—make a jungle you peer out of, suspicious-eyed, at the bustle around (this is also contrast of identities, the wild in the city, and immediacy, This and That juxtaposed directly. Everything is always many other things at once) done either with an arch,

RIVERSIDE, CALIFORNIA

or an avenue,

PERSHING SQUARE, LOS ANGELES

—to add a dimension to the field of vision, like wearing stereoscopic spectacles,

YALE

—or, most mysterious of all, to mark infinity. This view in New Haven, Connecticut,

NEW HAVEN

91

has the Atlantic at the end of it, in other words infinite air and sea. But the infiniteness is only fully realized if it is given a finite frame. (The perspective of houses in the street is not the same, because they are like a mathematical progression, i.e., although finite they are tending to infinity.) What the houses don't do, the great spreading leaves of the tree can, with their utter here-ness and finiteness. An arch over the road would do the same thing, but not so poignantly or so expressively. "Just a road" and "just a tree," but arranged, or a perception of an accidental arrangement, and it is the arranging, the exercise of the intellect to delight the emotions, which is one of the marks by which we are human. And conversely, if we refuse to select and discriminate and treat individual cases individually and apply different rules in different circumstances, we are sliding back—have already slid back—to bestiality. It is more difficult today, there are more pressures, more things to have to make choices about. That is the real price of progress. If we accept it, then our real reward is that we are that much more human, by choice, than we were before. We can choose to evolve.

6 | HALFWAY

By what may have seemed to be a roundabout route, I have tried to get to a simple two-part proposition:

First, the way to an expressive and exciting total environment is by the creation of separate identities with their own limits and laws. This is true equally of a city, a state, a continent. The whole continent should resemble a human body built up of innumerable different parts, each with its own identity (noses, fingernails, gall bladders) yet each forming an essential part of the whole. These identities need not resemble the traditional Western European types at all: they may be supermarket center, expressway, atomic plant, desert, air terminal. Nor are they made by use-zoning, which bears the same relation to identity as a robot does to the human body—a mechanical collection of parts, not a living thing. But sharp and distinct they must be; and a variety of each must be within reach of everyone. In the words of a memorable phrase from *Exploding Metropolis* (by the Editors of Fortune):

> The fact that there will remain thousands of acres of empty land in, say, Wyoming is not going to help the man living in Teaneck, New Jersey.

92   *Second*, the physical way to create these identities is to provide physical relationships and space sequences made up from the elements within them. Each identity will have different elements which can be arranged in different ways. Space sequences imply some kind of continuous space, and it is for this reason that the standard American gridiron plan is such a drawback. Curvy plans by themselves are no solution, for the Levittowns are as curved as you like. They are only one means to an end.

If these two can be grasped and applied, then any townscape or landscape problem becomes easy. That is why so much time has been spent on them, instead of on specific problems such as the relationship of expressways to city centers and the dispersal of ex-urban population. If a universal basis can be provided and understood, then the application to a particular problem comes from inside and is a feeling, living thing, instead of being applied from outside, coldly and rationally. A situation such as the smashing of an expressway through Boston's North End would simply not have arisen, because the people responsible would have taken account of the identities and run the roads around them, thus defining and accentuating rather than obliterating. The expressway would have had its own identity and it would simply have enhanced the contrast.

The quality of the specific solution depends on the quality of the individual designer and in the end cannot be taught; it can only be helped. But the basis rightness of the solution is something that I think can become common knowledge: and it is really absurdly simple, depending only on the real comprehension of these two propositions. The consequences of the propositions are indeed complicated, for they involve the terrific assumption that each place is different, that each case must be decided on its own merits, that completely different solutions may be needed for apparently similar cases. In other words, that nothing has a prejudged label: true freedom.

This complexity is natural (unlike the applied complexity of zoning regulations and by-laws) and works from inside outward; and the true planner will find it no more awkward to control than the complexity offered by the myriad working parts of his body when he walks into a restaurant and eats a meal.

What follows now is the further working out of some of these complexities, a ragbag of hints and solutions and unexplored potentials. But the book's main purpose is established—and had to be established in this circuitous, step-by-step way. If it has not been understood, then these will simply appear as a set of random observations; if it has been, then they will appear as naturally and organically multiform as the different shapes and sizes of the branches of a tree. The thing it is trying to show is not so much what to do—that is up to you—but to suggest the underlying principles of how to do it.

93

7 | MAKING THE ENVIRONMENT SPEAK

Identity is given by the total place—buildings and the spaces between them, and all the objects in the spaces. Often, the objects in the spaces are more important than the buildings: a street lamp or a sign or a traffic island can completely alter the character of a particular place. This does not mean that there should be rigid and dogmatic control by one person over everything that goes into a particular view: God forbid! But it does mean that this feeling for relationship needs to be practiced universally, so that when a row of parking meters is combined with a wall and the floor, it interlocks with what is there already, forms a new entity. Here is a piece of Marietta, Pennsylvania, which does exactly that:

MARIETTA

It is simply a matter of painting the wall white, of differentiating between road and sidewalk by a change in surface (asphalt and brick), of articulating the road space with white lines. The meters cease to become an imposition and become punctuation, the literal, modern equivalent of the old hitching post. The whole environment starts to speak.

The floor is terribly important, here. It is the necessary grammatical link which makes the separate buildings articulate. It can be the great unifying force, with a pattern as complex as the pattern of traffic in a city, or it can be an asphalt desert. Sometimes complexity is needed, sometimes unified simplicity. Louisburg Square in Boston is helped tremendously by having its traffic pattern expressed in the floor: static traffic on cobbles, pedestrians on the stone setts, through traffic on asphalt.

But Washington Square in New York needs the opposite effect to set off Stanford White's triumphal arch

BOSTON SQUARE

and redeem the heterogeneous mess that twentieth-century architects, ancient and modern, have made out of the edges. Instead of a babel of different kinds of floor surface it needs one vast sweep—perhaps of stone paving from side to side as has been done in Munich, with the seats and the big trees growing out of it with the least possible interference. It would not do in many places, and generally this sort of grand gesture is used too often. This is the one place where it is really needed.

Properly used, the floor can tell you everything about the pattern of road use by means of changes of surface and paint. There is no need for any lettered vertical signs at all. This corner of Pensacola has got the idea:

PENSACOLA

95

NEW ORLEANS FLOOR

And not only traffic information.

The old New Orleans street names, now neglected, have a much greater significance than simply being a picturesque relic. They make a town look lived-in, as the imaginative use of furniture makes a room look "lived-in." And every gesture like this adds to the store of urban humanity. Perhaps it is no accident that America, with the least humane cities in the world, should have the biggest urban crime problem in the world also.

Walls can be just as expressive. In this building in Detroit the result is not only a fire escape but an enrichment of the city.

DETROIT

And if that effect is accident, the fire escapes on the famous Hallidie building in San Francisco are unquestionably design,

SAN FRANCISCO

the exact boundary where architecture and townscape join. In fact, the wall or building and the floor should be able to melt together while keeping their identity. There should be not just street and building, but a constant interaction between them. Never mind the legal difficulties and the lines of demarcation between authorities, who are after all our own creation anyway: the environment is all one. For when the parts do mingle, the most magical effects occur. Look at this Charleston portico

CHARLESTON

not as a specimen of eighteenth-century architecture but for what it does to the space in the street—an experience as valid for 1960 as it was for 1760. Space

97

is netted inside it, there is simultaneously a building penetrating the street and a street penetrating the building. Not separate parts of the environment, but an integral, unified thing. A tree in Charleston does the same thing even more simply.

CHARLESTON

CRANBROOK

Yet I am sure that in some places a rule-bound person would say, "That's overhanging the sidewalk; lop it back."

Again, statues can be used as isolated commemorative objects, struck down without relationship, or they can flow together with the rest of the environment. Italian towns understand this perfectly. The panel of illustrations is a very special place (Cranbrook Academy, Bloomfield Hills, Michigan) with a very special sculptor (Carl Milles) but it makes the point. "Statues," "landscape" and "buildings" cease to be separate things; they are part of one greater identity, the whole place. And not a rarefied, esoteric place either: for the top of the water tower fits perfectly behind Eliel Saarinen's portico.

98

CRANBROOK

The negative side of this is that the environment should not be willfully prevented from speaking. This, and not tidy-mindedness or any puritan impulse, is the reason for saying that the clutter of street signs should be tidied up and integrated—*in some cases*. This might be true of this street corner in Portsmouth, New Hampshire, which is bedeviled by a set of inexpressive and contradictory signs and poles which make it im-

PORTSMOUTH

possible to read the space around—and this space, after all, is Portsmouth, its essence. But in other cases the mess and clutter *is* the essence; no two places are alike, no two solutions are the same. And what better place to prove it than Times Square?

TIMES SQUARE

Again, there are times when gas pumps need to be straightforward and (literally) shipshape, for example, on the quay at Marblehead, Massachusetts

MARBLEHEAD

and times when they need to be wrought around with every kind of ballyhoo—east of Phoenix, Arizona, on US 60-70, for instance.

PHOENIX

And look at how within this range on the same road a completely different place is created by an (accidental) juxtaposition of fewer and bolder forms—the storage tank and the Union sign.

PHOENIX

One should not look like the other, for they are different types of objects. Each should have its own place on US 60-70, each should be augmented consciously instead of being left to accident. And a completely different type of environment on US 60-70 should also be allowed its own individuality, instead of being grubbed up wholesale for a universe of views like Phoenix on page 101. Not one *or* the other, that is, not universal arcadia or universal roadtown, but both together and sufficiently near each other to be able to enjoy the contrast and offer a choice of environment.

PHOENIX

Vision is only one of the five senses. All the others can be used as aids and components in making the whole environment speak in this way, and the end of this chapter is simply a medley of non-visual sensations, to indicate the range waiting to be expressed. They can all be augmented, played with and counterpointed, in just the same way as we have done with visual experience.

—The noise of tires on wire mesh bridges across rivers, often from one state to another, giving an audible, nonliterary sign that a border has been crossed.

—The multiple thump of the flags around the (Washington) Memorial in Washington in a high wind, and the much lighter, staccato flapping of the flags on the Texaco and Sunoco stations.

—The feel of walls. Brick, rough concrete, ashlar, granite, mud.

—The accidentally heated sidewalks in New York where the subway ventilators come out.

—The blast from the klaxon of an unseen freight train on the Illinois prairie, like a supernatural organ.

—The pop records playing in the shops of Forty-Second Street, New York.

—The Brattleboro Klaxon. For some reason, on the day I was in this little Vermont town, the sound reverberated around the hills six or eight times. If this is a permanent effect, why not use it? Klaxon recitals, klaxons in canon, syncopated klaxons. We have never had so many exciting tools, and we have never had so little imaginative idea of what to do with them. Use everything, play the most universal and most magical of all games: create and act, don't just let universal goop happen to you and then give a miserable grin at the sick jokes.

8 | APPROPRI-ATENESS

Every object in the environment can help to make an identity by its intrinsic design, as well as by being related to its surroundings. And, just as the spaces between buildings are often more important than the buildings themselves in this business, so the apparently unimportant individual bits of street furniture can make or mar a whole town square. Each object need not be self-expressive in this way—and it is far better for it to be neutral than to try to achieve, artificially and laboriously, some kind of tickled-up expression. The thing it must not do is to express some other kind of environment altogether—the rustic seat in the metropolitan plaza—unless a deliberate shock is intended. Deliberate shocks are only effective if the pattern as a whole is coherent—the eighteenth-century folly in the orderly landscaped park. The over-all pattern is hardly coherent anywhere in the world today, least of all in America, and our job at the moment must be a basic kind of sorting out. The frills and *frissons* can come later; for the moment we have our hands overfull of bizarre accidents. In another century the problem might be reversed, as it was two hundred years ago: we just happen to be on the other limit of the pendulum's swing between order and chaos. Neither are virtues in themselves, they are just functional conditions, but the extraction of meaning and feeling out of a combination of the two is indeed a virtue.

If these objects can be made expressive in the right way (i.e., city-like objects in a city, suburb-like objects in a suburb, and so on), then the sense of identity is enriched and intensified. In at least one respect, America has a splendid tradition of street objects: most of her city furniture is truly metropolitan, just as most American cities are truly large-scale. The fire hydrants of New York and San Francisco are magnificent objects, and the old traffic lights in San Francisco stand up splendidly to the hurry and flux of city life.

SAN FRANCISCO

103

The same is true of details like the ship's bollard at the end of Canal Street in New Orleans,

and of an object like this Chicago water meter, every bit as worthy of attention as a Sullivan building.

104

A pair of almost identical street signs can convey subtly but quite definitely the difference between a city (San Francisco)

SAN FRANCISCO

and a small country town (Cambridge, near Saratoga Springs, New York).

CAMBRIDGE

The rural equivalent of this is harder to suggest, but this filling station on State 94 east of San Diego is as appropriate to a remote byway

SAN DIEGO

as the bold 66 station is to US 80 near El Paso—a set of photographs making the same point as the gas pumps in the last chapter.

TEXAS

SHELTERS

These wayside shelters in New Mexico east of Duncan have a no-nonsense straightforwardness about them whereas the design is usually killed with kindness—i.e., overprettiness.

The taut overriding rhythm of poles and wires is as appropriate to the Illinois prairie

ILLINOIS

as it is unwanted and obstructive in this New England view (Carmel, near Danbury, Connecticut).

CARMEL

Prettiness and fussiness in the wrong place is the curse of modern design. Good ideas like the center of Park Forest, Illinois, or the Kalamazoo Mall in Kalamazoo, Michigan, are devalued because their designers—with the best of intentions—throw every

107

kind of object into the newly created pedestrian space. The relief at having got rid of the motor cars is so great that the adjuncts of every kind of pedestrian activity are imported regardless of the nature of the place. It is not the activities that are wrong but the means of expression that are found for them. In the Mall at Kalamazoo, for example, there is a sandbox. Now this as an idea is admirable—somewhere for the kids to play safely, yet without being shut up, while the mums do the shopping. Yet it has simply been given the kind of treatment that would fit a sandbox in a back garden, and hence it looks fiddling and small-scale in the middle of a town street: just as out of place as a monumental sandbox would be in the back garden.

KALAMAZOO

PARK FOREST

A street lamp like this, which would be admirable in a subdivision or an intimate corner of a small town, is simply lost on its present site, which is in fact the civic center of New Orleans.

Small-scale or back garden techniques are sometimes misplaced out into the countryside as well as in the center of the town—and in America more than anywhere else the scale of the countryside is huge and menacing. The result is what occasionally happens with road landscaping (e.g., on US 90 east of Tallahassee) where pretty, small-scale planting looks ridiculous against the surrounding Deep-South scrub

NEW ORLEANS

108

woodland. A more subtle form of this prettification is the way pastel colors are used where no possible pastel effect can be obtained—inside a building as masculine in purpose and design as this, for example (the state fair auditorium in Raleigh, North Carolina).

RALEIGH

Even worse is the idea of painting pastel shades on gasoline tanks in the middle of the desert, as happens on US 66—of all places, as it is the most brutal and unaccommodating of American highways—near Gallup, New Mexico. There, the right and wrong way of doing it can be seen within a few miles: one set in greens and mauves, simply looking like storage tanks preposterously got up, the other set in sparkling white; appropriate to themselves, appropriate to the hard, direct, desert landscape, white globe against red mesa. The pastel shades might have been marvelous on another thing and in another place.

TANKS

The best place to look at the nuances of appropriateness is in street lettering. There is no one type of lettering which fits everywhere: once legibility and comprehensibility have been satisfied, the business of selection has just begun. Sometimes the sign is best left neutral, conveying information only. Most road signs are like this (Cambridge, New York):

CAMBRIDGE

109

110 Sometimes the information needs to be reinforced but not made expressive (San Diego):

But thereafter, there are as many varieties as there are types of information to be expressed. Each of these seven examples says what it is in the style of its lettering as well as in the meaning of the words—and not by adopting an applied style, but internally. Each is also, incidentally, completely appropriate to its site.

CLEVELAND

WASHINGTON, D. C.

SAN FRANCISCO

NEW HAVEN

NEW YORK CITY

NEW YORK CITY

If the hankering after character and expressiveness comes from outside without inner conviction, the result is like this:

DETROIT

which conveys no idea of speed, and is simply weak, flabby and half-hearted. If it is thought about too much from the head as a "design problem" and not enough from the heart, the result comes out like this,

BOSTON AND MAINE RAILROAD   NEW HAVEN RAILROAD

even though famous designers may have been responsible. In these two examples the idea of having a monogram got in the way of the monogram itself.

Finally, if the whole lot goes flabby there is a dissolution of all the types of lettering, slick or strict. Roadtown lettering is mechanical and loveless, but it *is* alive. If the life is taken out in a well-intentioned but misguided attempt to tidy up, the result is— Park Forest.

PARK FOREST

Appropriateness or is-ness or the quality of being itself can no more come from outside in objects than it can in people. The place that puts on good design for extraneous reasons is probably worse than all the others. It is pointless to try, the falsity will always show. In England we have a lot of highly qualified men fiddling around with pub design. From the results, about one out of ten knows what it is all about; the other nine look at the glossy magazines and never get **113** drunk. And you can always tell which is which.

9 | "AMENITY"

"When in doubt, build a mall, and the bigger the better" is in many ways the signature tune of urban improvement in the 1960's. Formality, more than anything else, is a good servant but a bad master in townscape design. It needs very careful handling, and it must never be used too often, otherwise it becomes hopelessly devalued. Each formal gesture has to really mean something, and each gesture must not be an alibi to prevent your having to think about something more intricate, but must grow inevitably out of the needs of the specific place. One grand axis in a city is fine; if there are six, the detached observer begins to suspect lack of invention. And the gridiron plan has insured that most American cities are already overloaded with the weakest kind of formal solution: the endless straight line endlessly repeated.

This overproduction of axes has meant that among all the bad examples there are some very good ones. The really good formal axis is one of the most typical American virtues, always on a huge scale and always freed from any kind of academic mealymouthedness. The prodigious axis from City Hall to the Art Gallery in Philadelphia is an example, and so is the pair of axes on which Washington is built. L'Enfant's star plan has become (or rather, always was) an unreal geometrical abstraction: the two axes west from the Capitol and south from the White House are meaningful, ample, and lead to significant objects. Nobody wants an axis focused on a slaughterhouse. And the point at which they intersect, the Washington Monument, is one of the best formal gestures anywhere. Simple, symbolic, making emotional as well as topographical sense, relying purely on the contrast between obelisk and ring of flags. No comment is needed on the government buildings blocking the way to the Lincoln Memorial.

AXIS

AXIS

MONUMENT

MONUMENT

Direct, expressive, economical, pierces to the heart: worth going three thousand miles to see. The corollary of this kind of plan is that Washington would be a much more exciting place if the surrounding mess of buildings was intricate, not geometrically gridded.

The sense of contrast, shock, suspense when you emerged from city to axis would then be many times stronger. The same effect ought to happen around the Jefferson arch on the riverside at St. Louis.

An expressway can be an admirable axis, because the lines of motion reinforce the topographical lines of force: this is the eastern approach to the state capitol at Tallahassee.

TALLAHASSEE

But defeat the lines of flow, obstruct them with fussy details, and the result is immediately bathos—for example, another state capitol, at Harrisburg, with a very fine axis frittered away by one or two tiny details.

HARRISBURG

Curiously enough, with so much misplaced formality, some great formal opportunities are missed, and some existing formal layouts are cruelly maltreated. New Orleans is a good place to have a look at this. It has a number of decent buildings (and one very good one, the library) arranged in a decent formal relationship to form a civic center.

116

Yet the result is implacably dull. Why? Partly, I fear, because the whole idea of a separate "civic center," another fearful consequence of use-zoning, is stillborn. Town life must be all mixed up, the civic and administrative buildings must be part of the town. When they are, the two charge each other up, and almost every courthouse square in America is the proof of it. The shops and saloons have more custom, the impersonal offices are humanized.

But the failure in New Orleans is also in the site. There was no organic need for a formal gesture just there, away at the back of everything, near the railway station. Paradoxically, a formal gesture needs to be more organically placed than anything else, just because of its artificiality. There must be an absolute need for just that shape in just that place with just those buildings. New Orleans has got an axis like that, wedded to its function in the city: Canal Street. Yet perversely, the end of it is blocked—the grand gesture which is crying out to be made, of ships and row after row of steps and ramps down to the water at the end of the street, peters out in traffic circles and shrubs (and a desperate, arrowed notice saying "for view of river"). On all the other parts of the New Orleans waterfront, the unexpected mess and informality of the river is good (or could be made to be: the best way would be a wandering here-and-there walkway on the roofs of the wharves). Just at this one spot the big gesture was really needed, an open-handed "Here I am, come and take me."

CANAL STREET

That is an unrealized formal grand gesture. New Orleans had a delightful formal gesture of another sort which it has just thrown away. Some way west of Canal Street is a little plaza called Lee Circle: small, elegant, in the right position to act as a focus. If anything should have been firmly and formally built up, this should. Yet it has been allowed to disintegrate into a shambles of parking lots and unrelated buildings with the Doric column sitting disconsolately in the middle.

LEE CIRCLE

An axis does not have to be wide and big. It can often be more effective by being deliberately constricted and narrow and irregular—the tension between apparent waywardness and the concealed direction and purpose, threading through the labyrinth. Such an axis could be made to exist in New Orleans between the civic center and the river and help to rework the imposing buildings back into the fabric of the city. It would run approximately down the line of Natchez Street, arrowed in the photograph; it is almost there already, and it would come out directly on the center of the Louisiana State building. The effect would be of an irregular-sided slit straight through the crowded old town to the completely different environment beyond.

NATCHEZ STREET

119 In fact, the straightforward, even-width axis focusing directly on a building should be just the starting point, the first step, for the townscaper. (Most of the time, today, if he manages to get that far he thinks himself a genius.) It is to townscape what simple four-four time is to music. Just one simple example will do, for once the idea is grasped the permutations are endless. If you go up the New Haven Green and into the main entrance at Yale you focus not on Harkness Tower, which is what you expect, but on a smaller, turreted building.

But you are expecting the Harkness building. What's happened? Immediately, tension, intrigue, the conflict between the axis that ought to be there and the one that actually is. A few steps further and the mystery is explained, with Harkness Tower peering around the corner.

Simple, but it never fails; and it has nothing to do with Neo-Gothic detail or cozy, turfed courtyards. The principle is universal and could apply just as easily to water towers or oil derricks or atomic factories.

The other two traditional components of "urban amenity"—open space and historic buildings—have the same requirement. They must be needed in the town, organically, where they are and for what they are. As museum pieces or isolated public parks they are worse than useless, like an area of dead flesh in a live body. A town square without bums has something very wrong with it, because the bums know instinctively what we have to learn so laboriously and with so much effort—that is, whether a place feels right. Parks and old buildings must never be in inverted commas: they must always appear natural and unaffected, worked into the landscape, there to be used. Brunswick, Georgia, has been mentioned before for its trees. Its plan must be one of the oddest in America: it started on the pattern of Savannah, with chains of squares

but somehow the roads got wider and the squares got smaller, so that they are left as little pocket-handkerchief indentations in the street-line,

and there they all are today, perfect informal urban parks, mixed in with the town's life yet leafy oases at the same time.

Those are four illustrations of the same tiny square yet they produce four quite different townscape impressions. The contrast of "outside" (the little pocket or incident in the street view) and "inside" (the bustling world seen from behind a jungle screen) is a townscape manual in itself. Yet, on a zoning map, any old scrubby patch of grass would have done. (These photographs, be it noted, were all taken in January.) The same thing, the contrast between inside and outside on a tiny scale, happens in the little park at the back of City Hall in Charleston.

But the parks need not be tiny. Each place has its own needs: as long as the solution meets the specific needs it does not matter what form it takes. Boston Common is an enormous park, just right for where it is, tying all the parts of the city together in a way that—in that particular instance, because the sides are so disparate—a sequence of buildings never could.

120

BOSTON COMMON

Appropriate to the scale of the Common—the steps and bollards are metropolitan too.

BOSTON COMMON

Yet just at the back of the Common, in the old town, is a tiny churchyard. In its specific position it is just right too, a breathing space from the crowded narrow streets.

BOSTON

121

More seats would help, but not fewer gravestones, for these reinforce the contrast in a most telling way, not in the least invalid because it is metaphysical rather than purely visual. The environment has got to speak to us in every way at once.

Equally, a large park can be a frightening monument to sterility, like the whole of Chicago's Lakeside excluding the first few yards from the water's edge. After a few steps you think, very nice: now some buildings, please, to show that city and lake belong together. But it just goes on and on, and in the most unpleasant, unrelated way: busy roads, featureless grass, rail tracks. From Michigan Avenue to the lake the actual count in terms of paces—and a dreary walk it is, too—is as follows:

100 PACES	*scrubby gardens*
100 PACES	*rail tracks*
120 PACES	*parking lot*
25 PACES	*road*
300 PACES	*grass and trees to formal patterns*
40 PACES	*road*
70 PACES	*grass*
755	

In this half-mile of "amenity," only the last seventy paces are at all pleasant. For the rest, I'd much rather walk up North Clark; at least you can get a drink there.

And of course small parks are no use if they are sterilized. Here again in Chicago is an overofficious little patch of deadness,

CHICAGO

hideously fenced in (if fences are needed, they ought not to look like that), plastered with notices: "No Dogs," "No Ball Games." What self-respecting kid would want to make use of it after that? It looks as though it were conceived in hate and despite: "Well, we have to give these people somewhere to sit, so let's make it as unpleasant as possible." It is not always the overt acts of rudeness and brutality which last longest or hurt deepest.

With historic buildings the only thing to do is to knit them into the town and not segregate them. The parallel with not committing your old grandmother to an institution is a fair one. The rhythm needed is illustrated most easily by places which have frankly nineteenth-century and frankly twentieth-century buildings side by side, as long as the juxtaposition is done sensitively, i.e., as long as the two are in relationship. Some examples are well known, like Louis Kahn's art gallery at Yale,

YALE

but the same point is made anonymously by the cheerful mixture of styles on Nob Hill in San Francisco.

NOB HILL

The environment, past and present, is all one, and it can no more be isolated and chopped up than the human body can.

The way these three apparently isolated subjects (formal gesture, urban open space, historic buildings) interact can be best shown in two examples of urban improvement, one very good and the other very bad. The bad one is the recently created Independence Mall in Philadelphia, a vast formal axis galloping off to nowhere, focused on a building (Independence Hall) which is too small to stand up to it and which is dominated anyway by a skyscraper behind and off-center.

PHILADELPHIA

Worse still is the historical zoo that is being constructed at the back of Independence Mall in which the monuments stand in landscaped grounds like gooney-birds, sterile and unrelated, to be looked at as museum specimens. The bums don't use the prairie barrenness of Independence Mall—they stay in the sleazy but live Franklin Square, nearby—and neither does anyone else. It is all unreal paper planning, the creation at enormous cost of an elaborate substitute for urban life. The often-derided Colonial Williamsburg has a far more organic pattern than this.

Enough said. A look at Boston shows how this kind of thing can be done to enhance the vitality of a city, not steam-roll it away. With a title like Paul Revere Mall (built in 1934) you expect the worst: everything in inverted commas and no life at all. Yet in fact it is quite different. If the same feeling for people and thought had gone into Independence Mall, that Philadelphia ice floe would be a much happier place. Paul Revere Mall is part of the Freedom Trail, which makes it an even more unlikely candidate for a living part of the city, and joins the Old North Church with Bulfinch's beautiful and little known church of St. Stephen. It does so through the middle of a block, a method which must be one of the prime levers in winning back the American city for the pedestrian. This belongs to the next chapter—everything belongs to every chapter—but to anticipate it, the answer is

124

not all pedestrians and no cars (that is sterility) but a balance of both—superimposed systems, in fact.

The experience begins down Hull Street, with the Old North Church at the end of it.

The historic building here is not isolated, it just happens quite naturally as part of an ordinary working street. By accident, it is not quite on the axis, something which immediately adds to the interest. You still get the formal value of the view, and there is also a tiny chink of light at one side which draws you on—continuous, not isolated space. That is the beginning of the Mall, but it does not show itself

all at once. You have to go down a narrow brick-paved passage first, heightening the build-up, making the eventual view

that much more effective. It is, exactly, like building up or slowing down the even tempo of a piece of music or an act of love. When you get there you are on a tiny belvedere—only two or three steps, but enough to give the "here and there" effect. Then the Mall opens out, formal but humane, exactly on the axis of St. Stephen's.

But St. Stephen's is not exactly on the axis of the Mall. The street pattern has meant that it is twisted by just a few degrees, one more addition in richness and subtlety. There is another very odd thing about this Mall. There are *people* in it, even on a November afternoon, enjoying themselves. And a lot of this is due to the humane details, and the freedom from hard surfaces and officious notices. The floor is brick and stone, comfortable, patched, the walls are brick— only nine feet high, but enough to give the sense of enclosure and unity. With a wire fence the effect would have been quite different. There are plenty of trees, and seats under them (how many "improvements" have trees with no seats, seats with no trees, or trees zoned at one end and seats zoned at the other? A terribly simple thing, yet a microcosm of the whole problem). When this kind of thought and care is provided, people come rushing up to complete it. When soured administrators talk sadly about creating something that is unwanted and unused, all it really means is that they have created the wrong thing or done the right thing in the wrong way. On this November afternoon the sun was coming in obliquely to light up one side—the bricks insuring that whatever sun there was was reflected and held, just as the seats- and-trees insure in summer that there will be maximum shade. From the care taken over the other details I would say that this is deliberate too. And the North

126

Enders move round the walls with the sun, playing cards, little knots of five or six people

BOSTON

being themselves, enjoying their city as naturally as though it were Rome or Naples. In fact, as most of the people in the North End are Italian, a capacity for urban enjoyment may be born in them. But that is not the whole story: the capacity is born in everybody, and it is the townscaper's job to bring it out and make it flower. It may take many different forms but the basic need is always there. Humanity, thank goodness, never quite loses. The last picture in this chapter expresses, better than anything else I found in America, people enjoying their city.

The time was Christmas morning, the place Pershing Square in the center of the unfairly derided city of Los Angeles, the place that everyone says has no center. There is *no* city that cannot provide amenity of this sort—it costs the same as inhumanity and regulation; all that it needs is love. And as soon as it is provided, then people will use it. Corporate life is being created here as surely as individual life is created in the womb.

LOS ANGELES

10 | CRACKING THE GRIDIRON: PEDESTRIAN'S WORLD

To achieve space sequences and any sort of unity there must be some alteration and variation in the standard, regular, evenly spaced gridiron. To achieve a proper balance between man and motorcars in big cities it is going to be necessary to provide a system of walkways for pedestrians which would separate but not segregate them from the other race that people become when equipped with four tires and a steering wheel. These two aims are largely complementary, and if used together could provide a nongridiron pedestrian network superimposed on the present city plans, much as the pedestrian network in Venice is superimposed on the canals. The third dimension, i.e., vertical separation, is the most important element in providing this network, but not the only one; and the aim is not to put cars out of sight all the time, for urban life would soon be very dull without them. The aim as always should be to try to provide a true choice of environment.

First, an anthology of ways of cracking the gridiron. The simplest way is to block it *tout court* by a building like Grand Central Station, which is why Park Avenue is quite different from any other street in New York.*

NEW YORK

This is not often practicable and in any case, by itself, does not produce a space sequence. If a building at the end of a street is askew, however (just like St.

128

* Since I wrote this the view has changed again, and Grand Central is overshadowed by the Pan American Building. A pity, because the termination was exactly right as it was.

Stephen's, Boston, in the last chapter), a very different effect is produced. The eye is

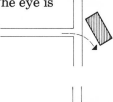

not

led around the corner; it is a very elementary kind of come-on. This is the effect of the block of buildings at Portsmouth, New Hampshire, which includes the Athenaeum. The curved street on the right-hand side is clearly going to lead you on somewhere else,

yet at the same time the decorative pilasters of the Athenaeum itself hold you to the axis until the very last moment.

PORTSMOUTH

Tension and movement, hence a memorable sequence, hence a unique identity: no other place in America is quite like that.

This effect, simultaneously stopping and leading on, can be done without blocking the street at all. The building can have the traffic going right through it, sitting on stilts or pilotis: or it can get an effect simply by taking in the sidewalk. This church in Charleston, North Carolina (St. Michael's), does it beautifully, helped also by the fact that the road narrows anyway. Here, there is both stop and come-on,

129

CHARLESTON

and a sophisticated, intellectual thrill as well from the knowledge that both stop and come-on are provided by the same architectural element (a four-column Doric portico) turned at right angle to itself. It is like discovering an entirely new dimension in a friend you thought you knew completely.

The same thing is done much more simply by this angled building on a corner site in Whitewater, Wisconsin,

WHITEWATER

which takes you round a bend in the road by the simplest possible device, i.e., with a hole in its ground floor.

WHITEWATER

Here, note the effect of the corner pillar, making a frame, accentuating the "there" around the corner. If a simple cantilevered overhang had been used the result would have been much less dramatic. That is the basic reason behind the proscenium arch in the theatre. (If you have theatre-in-the-round you gain many other things but you lose the effect of the frame.)

Even more simply, a building angled at 45° to the street immediately gets away from the rigid geometry. This delightful one is in San Francisco.

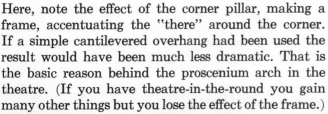

SAN FRANCISCO

There are other sorts of come-on. One of the best is something completely different at the end of the street, from which the eye can infer what is going to happen there. An ordinary street in Charlestown, Boston, blocked by the expressway, is transformed by what is at the end of the view: masts.
Similarly, the ship at the end of New Orleans' Canal Street means that you infer immediately what is going on: there is no need for a sign to tell you.

BOSTON

The opposite effect is this road end at Bratenahl next to Cleveland, where an unintentionally ironic pair of signs contains no hint

CLEVELAND

that what is over the bank (which you would be bound to come on, of course, if the stop sign weren't there) is in fact the strange, unexpected turbulence of Lake Erie.

CLEVELAND

If the third dimension is added, the come-on can become a come-on-up-and-over. A single railing can do it, like the one in this street in Prescott, Arizona, giving a hint of what is beyond the brow, articulating the landscape.

PRESCOTT

More complicated and more impressive is the effect of the little shelter on top of Duquesne Heights, Pittsburgh. Seen from a distance it is as regular as the Portsmouth Athenaeum, first simply as a puzzling object at the end of the street, framing

PITTSBURGH

and beckoning, then recognizable as a shelter. Here the mind

PITTSBURGH

gives the eye a few common-sense directions. A shelter on the brow of a hill must mean that there is something worth looking at beyond it. And when you get close, of course, there is something: first framed—the final holding in and holding back before the revelation—

PITTSBURGH

and then exposed fully.

PITTSBURGH

This experience is emphatically not the same as a straightforward walk up the hill to a view over the top. This bit of the environment has been stressed, charged up. Every bit of the environment could be, if we would let it.

A more familiar example—the steps opposite the U. N. Building in New York, bridging Forty-second Street, shows incidentally the richness of sensations that have accumulated accidentally. The sequence depends, once again, on going up and down and on using some kind of curved line. Beginning on First

133

Avenue, the first view shows the complexity, the result of blocking a view and curving the foreground. Handrail, steps, street lamp, bits of buildings beyond, lettering on the right-hand side. Halfway

NEW YORK

up, and the relationship has quite changed. Straight steps would not have done it, nor would a flat curve. It is the three-dimensional combination just as it is in Gothic or Baroque architecture. Skyline buildings have gone, handrail is going, but the street lamp and the top railing are brought into an

NEW YORK

exciting relationship which is not simply geometrical. It is also the fine-art world of the handrail versus the commercial and legal world of the lamp and the unclimbable railing on the right. From the top, traffic, however dense, is no psychological worry because you are above it, free to stop and go as you like. But also, the place would not be nearly so effective if the traffic weren't there at all.

NEW YORK

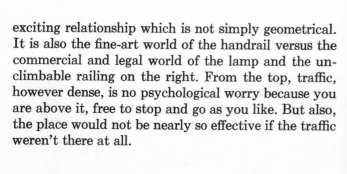

The reverse of this walk is quite different. Even the view of Forty-second Street seen the other way is completely different: looking this time out of the city instead of into it. The view

NEW YORK

looking down on the inscription is not just the same experience run backward: it is a different space and a different sequence (whereas a walk down an uninflected block in most main streets is the same forward or backward). The view toward the U. N. Building, in fact, hardly looks as though it were in the same city at all. It is also a splendid example of the range of

NEW YORK

effects available in the twentieth-century city, effects that we never use because we never juxtapose and bring into relationship: the change in scale between ashcans and the bank of windows, the mirror effect of windows themselves, reflected buildings behind the viewer—this, used deliberately, could be the basis of a splendid range of echo-effects (e.g., this view of Kahn's AFL-CIO building in Philadelphia)—

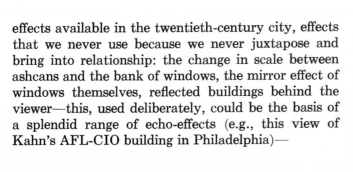

PHILADELPHIA

the contrast in textures, ashcan/railing/glass, the contrast in purpose between the ordinary office buildings and the vast glass slab, the implied contrast of national and international frailty. Concentrated here in fact is a whole set of contrasts, and a set capable of being enjoyed and observed from a pedestrian network which is separated from motor traffic but not isolated from it. The motor traffic in fact provides the biggest and most exciting contrast of all. In this tiny bit of New York the choice is available: the usual sidewalks and the pedestrian network.

Here is the townscape key to making American big cities expressive and humane. And unlike problems such as sorting out an exurban bit of Connecticut into distinct areas, it is a comparatively easy thing to start. The aim should be a superimposed pedestrian network, irregular and humane, with plenty of wayward human touches to hang on to: a kind of messy, untidy carpet to the big buildings all around and the regimented stop-and-go of the traffic. The wide sterility of a landscaped mall is the last thing that is needed, except in very special circumstances.

There are plenty of hooks on which to hang such a system, and once begun it would easily spread because it makes economic sense as well as townscape sense. Most cities still have their mid-block alleys, and not many are as sheer and exciting (but for this purpose almost unusable) as Chicago's.

CHICAGO

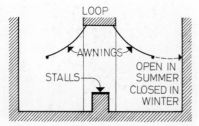

Chicago would have to use them as an element in the other side of the game, macro-city not micro-city. Where it could start might be in roofing over some of the streets under the Loop, such as Wabash Avenue, with awnings under which any kind of open-air life could flourish. In winter the whole lot could be centrally heated.

This Louisville street has something of the same idea.

LOUISVILLE

But most alleys are more tractable than Chicago's, and can be converted into pedestrian territory quite easily. Maiden Lane in San Francisco is the famous example. But it is far too affected and *soigné* to be any use in the average city center. What has happened at the back of the Alcoa Building in Pittsburgh has more relevance. There, alleys called Montous Way and Strawberry Way are just beginning to be rescued from the trash cans and pointless squalor—one or two shops have opened up. All over America, there are fragments like this waiting to be knit into a pedestrian pattern which could be as exciting and meaningful as that of Venice. Sometimes they are cozy backwaters, like Elfreth's Alley in Philadelphia

PHILADELPHIA

137

NEW ORLEANS

or streets which have already been made pedestrian, like Pirates Alley in New Orleans.

But a few streets like this are not enough: they must be connected and made into convenient short cuts; easier, quicker and pleasanter than motoring-and-parking. Footpaths through big office blocks is one way of doing it, as in the Esso Building and the Tishman Building in New York.

TISHMAN BUILDING

There will always be some place to start making a sequence. A tiny town like Tamaqua on US 309 in the coal-mining part of Pennsylvania has parallel main streets with the usual amount of vacant land between them. These could easily become one-way, with the space between them pedestrian—open space, shops, what you will.

This is mostly a metropolitan job. It is more than ever needed in the deserts that result, with the best

138

will in the world, from most of our urban-redevelopment projects—a few tall blocks standing around disconnectedly and disconsolately in a tangle of roadways, parked cars and scraps of grass. The organic pattern that any place must have has been completely disregarded, and one imaginary drawing can stand for them all.

EXPLODING METROPOLIS

Another, called the Gateway Center, alas not so imaginary, has been put up in Pittsburgh to general applause. At present, it is a collection of stone-dead big buildings.

PITTSBURGH

Yet this could be transformed by a single-story pedestrian carpet—shops, bars, seats. The cars and roads would still be underneath, the carpet could have holes cut in it for trees and to add to the contrast by occasional views of the traffic. The carpet need not be bound by the grid or any geometrical layout, it need not be the same height all over: a complete, unexplored new dimension of town design. Imagine the Hyde Park blocks (page 25) united and made humane by this kind of thing.

139

One American city has got a connected, continuous pedestrian pattern as well as the ordinary streets. But this time the pedestrians are down, not up, on river banks twenty feet below street level. The city is San Antonio, which has the San Antonio river looping right through the center. At one time it was due to be roofed over as a storm sewer; it was instead laid out as a linear garden, in the 1930's, and still remains the best example of urban landscaping in America. All it lacks is more variety in the kind of objects—i.e., kiosks, cafés, bars, a few entrances from offices and shops. The fussiness and overprettiness which is the bane of so much urban designing (see Kalamazoo on page 108) is almost absent here.

SAN ANTONIO

And it is a *sequence*, not an isolated park. Check the position of the Alamo National Bank in the next three views as it gradually gets nearer and nearer in the background.

This is not a set of conventional pretty bits, but a connected, organic pattern: a townscape sensation as good as any in the world. The Alamo Bank is the "there" to the "here" of the river bank. And just as the traffic, seen from the bridge near the U. N. Building, added another dimension to the experience, so the various terms of the upper world prevent this sequence from being just a beautifully landscaped walk.

SAN ANTONIO

Gasworks and electricity substations and billboards and skyscrapers all appear without breaking the flow because the visual limits of each is defined—there is no smudging or blurring. And, of course, the ordinary city gridiron gains immeasurably through having a sudden magical world beneath it.

SAN ANTONIO

140

San Antonio's riverside is thirty years old now. Nothing so good on this scale has been done since— and although San Antonio was very lucky to have such a river going through it, every city has some kind of remarkable feature in it to be caught hold of. Chicago itself has its forgotten subterranean river banks, a fantastic Piranesian world which it ignores completely.

If it were brought into the town pattern the treatment would have to be completely different from San Antonio's—each place makes its own rules. No walks and comfortable seats here: everything as bleakly metropolitan as Chicago itself.

In fact, one bit of the riverside has been brilliantly utilized in the last few years. The walk along the front of the Chicago Sun-Times Building is not just a promenade, though it could have been. To start with, it turns a sharp corner,

before running along the front of the Sun-Times: a straight-forward entry would have been far less dramatic (and whether

this was accident or necessity rather than conscious design is irrelevant. The important thing is to note the effect and be prepared to use it). The offices of the Loop, meanwhile, make up a "there" of the most dramatic kind

143

while seen on the left through the window are the printing presses.

CHICAGO

The immediate contrast of this—extreme inside (printing presses, bowels of buildings) and extreme outside (Loop skyline) juxtaposed—sets up a rhythm which projects you to the end of the path like a missile. There, the Wrigley Building takes over, first as a skyline flanked by the fins of the Sun-Times.

CHICAGO

A short link where the sequence breaks down because of a fussy garden (not because it is a garden, but because it is fussy, and so loosens the rhythm and scale of the rest), then the extraordinary white glazed world of the Wrigley.

The end of this is a sophisticated accident, that after the abundance of open-air, the closing view is seen through a sheet of glass: an "inside" effect where it is least expected. But halfway along, something even more unexpected happens. The high level bridge linking the two blocks becomes enough of a magnet to make the walker look up

CHICAGO

CHICAGO

so that his axes are already disoriented. Then, if he looks down to the floor at exactly the same point, he gets not reassurance but a much more terrifying dissolution: the iron grille reveals far below—at a level where the eye, from outside impressions, does not expect anything to be—an underground road. The simultaneous effect, over and under, is unforgettable. It topples the viewer's senses as aerobatics topples an aircraft's gyro instruments.

The reverse of this walk is just as much out of the ordinary. To start with, it seems (visually) impossible to get in at all. The Wrigley window reflects so much that the small hole in the center seems to be one more reflection.

CHICAGO

Thereafter the direct way is not by the riverside but through the Sun-Times Building. And here, with a double counterpoint, the left-hand view is of the river through the print machinery. So from an outside that has gone inside you look through a true inside to a true outside. And this is no esoteric or over-refined impression: it can be had for the asking—and the creating. For every few yards like this, in America, how many tens of thousands of miles are there of screaming

145 monotony?

11 | SORTING OUT THE CRAP

If the whole of the American scene were up to the level of the examples in the last few chapters, there would be no need for this book. Alas, it is probably the most characterless and least differentiated mess that man has ever made for himself. It is not at all what American man is doing but how he is doing it. The Atlantic seaboard could be a metropolitan area five hundred miles long and look magnificent—if the area were sorted out into different identities and were not an amorphous sprawl over a dozen states. The identities must include countryside, lots of it, right in the middle of a metropolitan area. Mobility and dispersal are fine; but let them be directed, given life and identity, clear boundaries and uniqueness. Then indeed a fragment of Philadelphia could be planted high up the Susquehanna with benefit; the corollary would be that most of Chester or Montgomery counties would stay truly rural. No restriction whatsoever is intended on the "what." All the parts of present-day American life, from the Howard Johnsons to the plutonium plant, can get along together as long as they don't run into and blur one another—zoned not by use but by character—and as long as each area contains a balance of different characters and identities. One exurban area at the moment contains subdivisions, countryside, roadtown, expressways, airfields, old communities. It still would contain the elements, but grouped, not scattered broadcast. The principles of grouping and creating identity are what this book has tried to suggest, and it has done so at such length because the elementary ideas of sequence and relationship are largely missing from America today.

The organic pattern of a whole countryside would be this: each unit—"subdivision," "highway interchange," "roadtown"—would be built up with all its parts in relationship and every bit of it done according to its own specific character (roadlike in roadtowns, country-like in the real country, and so on). Here the identity is built up with individual objects. These units are then fitted together to form a complete environment using the same ideas of sequence and relationship: the larger identity built up of relationships between the parts. So:

At present (say a highway interchange

UNIT

and the cafés, gas stations around it)

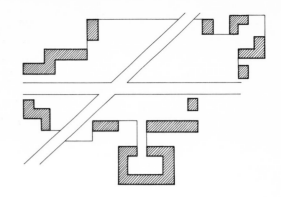

SUBDIVISION

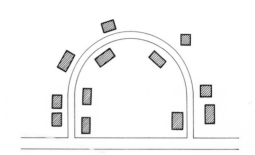

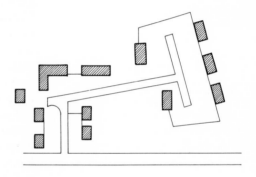

**GROUP OF SUBDIVISIONS,
HIGHWAY INTERCHANGE
AND ROADTOWN**

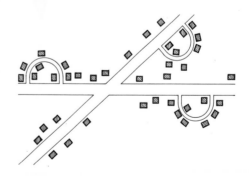

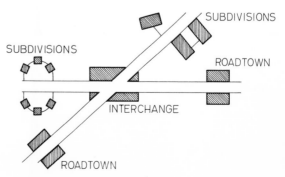

147

All the things that were there before, but grouped and related. Put more simply, no man-in-environment is an island.

This is a purely abstract and undirected bit of exurbia, though that is going to be the pattern of more and more of America. It applies to a metropolitan area in a slightly different way.

At present   As it should be

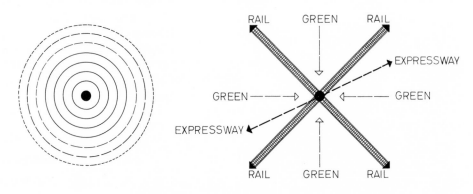

English practice would be to surround the city with a green belt. With American scale that would be pointless, and would lead to a tiny green ribbon and an enormous area of cut-off exurbia beyond it. The only hope is to allow expansion freely in some directions, restrict it utterly in others to polarize the metropolitan area. The natural directions to choose are the railway lines and old roads*—with the eventual aim of creating not an overwhelming commuting traffic but a continuous to-and-fro along the line in both directions. This is what now happens in exurbia anyway. These lines would not be continuous towns, but would be polarized and given identities in the same way that the polarization attempts to give identity to a metropolitan region. Thus the final pattern

would not be   but something like

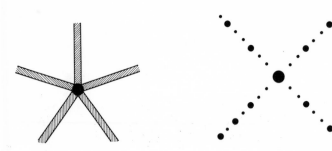

—varied to fit the individual needs and requirements. The land in between the polarized directions should be kept open and rural so that eventually the city center would have countryside at its doorstep, for if a city

---

* Not expressways—otherwise they stop being express. They must be used for inter-city travel, not as aids to commuting.

148

decided on the directions for expansion it could piece-meal buy up developed or derelict land in the wedges as it came on the market and make a set of parks which would gradually coalesce into a coherent green wedge.

There is no reason why these nucleated cities should not stretch across the whole continent. Here is how one small section might work, between Chicago and Fort Wayne, where US 30 and the main railroad running parallel make a natural direction stretching to Pittsburgh. Built-up Chicago ends quite suddenly between Gary and New Chicago, with open fields up to the houses. This edge should be preserved. Thereafter, the diagram shows the degree of expansion which could occur. The corollary of this is that the wedges on either side of this stay green right up to the Chicago limit.

1.   •   new "village"
2.   ⊙   enlarge existing scatter
3.   ⊕   existing town or village, slight expansion or leave alone

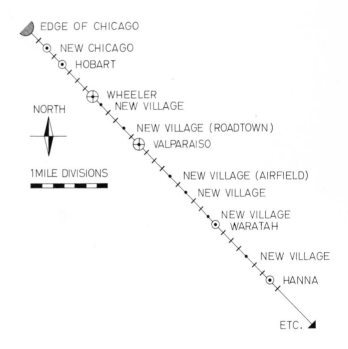

Inside the metropolitan area a similar defining and separating must go on.

Not   but

149   The lines of new expressways and their natural use of curves can be of immense value here. So, paradoxically, can parking lots, provided they are grouped and define boundaries. Here is a section of Los Angeles which is almost all parking lots. It looks like this:

LOS ANGELES

and on the ground, like this:

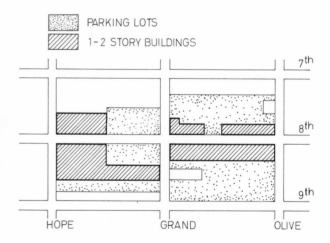

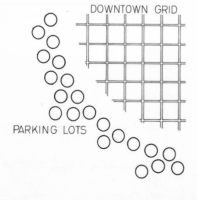

This area does by a happy accident define physically the edge of downtown Los Angeles. With nothing more than a few trees, the area could begin to define Los Angeles visually also. More parking lots could prolong the boundary, make the parked car a thing to be welcomed, not feared, in a joint private and municipal enterprise.

And, gradually, a city such as Los Angeles could have its constituents defined, then each constituent could

have its identity enhanced in its own way, The down-town grid of through motor roads could quite easily end up like this.

The whole of America, from Pacific to Atlantic, could be built up organically and sensitively, just as a human body is made up of molecules making cells, making organs and limbs. At the moment America is a great big heap of artifacts—the most varied and exciting heap that the world has ever seen, dumped down in the most monotonous and dreary way that the world has ever seen. If they could be given pattern, the result would be the most varied, exciting and unregimented set of places that the world has ever seen, each with its own internal order coming out of its own specific needs; perhaps similar to the next place, perhaps completely different.

It is, frankly, a vision; there's no point in half measures. But it is a vision that could be carried out in a hundred million tiny stages. Any of them would be an improvement, any of them could be carried out independently of any others. That is part of the vision too: no grand superimposed plan, politically unworkable and temperamentally unpracticable, but a million gestures of self-help. As long as the gestures practice relationship and sequence and identity, they are bound to come out right, and the more disparate they are, the better. So the "how" by which this might be achieved is as empirical as the thing itself. Sometimes it might be a state planning commission, sometimes a group of citizens, sometimes a single property-owner who would make the first gesture in an area—a single piece of preserved countryside, a new subdivision, a courthouse square, an urban renewal project. If the idea has anything in it, then it will spread of its own. If not, then no amount of imposition will make it work, and there would be no point in trying.

One further step could be taken immediately, and that is a pilot scheme to look at a town and its countryside together, in terms of sorting out identities, defining boundaries, exploring townscape and landscape potentialities. There have been surveys galore, but never like this: a survey trying to give a character map of a whole region.

It would best be a medium-size town between 50,000 and a quarter of a million—Lancaster, Pennsylvania, or Muncie, Indiana (already famous for another sort of survey, Lynd's *Middletown*), or Albuquerque or San Diego or Lansing. It would have to be a rapid survey, sketching in rather than exploring street-by-street, if it is not to get bogged down in a welter of information. It must be as compelling as a novel, as persuasive as a political tract. It must have general application without losing the ability to solve particular cases. Above everything else, it must be fun—fun to do, fun to write, fun to read. It in many

151

152 ways is the necessary sequel to this book. The job is necessary and urgent. If the face of America is not to disappear in a welter of nonidentity, the time to act is right now. The need for visual identity is there, the tools with which visual identity can be created are there. All that is lacking is the elementary know-how to make the tools express the needs. A whole new world of excitement and fulfillment is waiting, implicit in the wonderful variety of American sites and in the wonderful variety of material that the twentieth century has made available.

ABOUT THE AUTHOR IAN NAIRN was born on August 24, 1930, in Bedford, England. After receiving a BA in Mathematics from Birmingham University, he served three years in the RAF as a jet fighter pilot. In 1954, he decided to devote his time to architecture. He was a contributor to *The Exploding Metropolis* (compiled by the Editors of *Fortune*), and has been an editor of *Outrage*, *Counter-Attack*, and (currently) the *Architectural Review*, and is the Architectural Correspondent of the *Daily Telegraph*. His works include *Your England*, *Guide to Modern Buildings in London* and *Nairn's Guide to London*. The present book is the result of a 10,000 mile trip through the United States in 1959-1960 under a Rockefeller Foundation grant administered by the University of Pennsylvania.